BARANGAY TO BROADWAY

Filipino American Theater History

WALTER ANG

Published in 2018 by Walter Ang
Erie, Pennsylvania, United States of America
filipinoamericantheater@gmail.com

Hardcover ISBN: 978-0-9996865-0-8
Paperback ISBN: 978-0-9996865-1-5
Ebook   ISBN: 978-0-9996865-2-2

Library of Congress Control Number: 2018901888

Publisher's Cataloging-in-Publication Data:
　　Names: Ang, Walter Ong, author.
　　Title: Barangay to Broadway : Filipino American theater history / Walter Ang.
　　Description: Includes bibliographical references and index. |
　　　　Erie, PA : Walter Ang, 2018.
　　Identifiers: ISBN 978-0-9996865-0-8 (hardcover) |
　　　　ISBN 978-0-9996865-1-5 (pbk.) |
　　　　ISBN 978-0-9996865-2-2 (ebook) |
　　　　LCCN 2018901888
　　Subjects: LCSH Filipino American theater. |
　　　　Filipino Americans in the performing arts. |
　　　　Asian American theater—History. |
　　　　BISAC PERFORMING ARTS / Theater / History & Criticism |
　　　　SOCIAL SCIENCE / Ethnic Studies / Asian American Studies
　　Classification: LCC PN2270.F54 .A54 2018 |
　　　　DDC 792.08995073—dc23

Contents

Introduction   *1*

1 Entertainment (1900s–1950s)   *5*
Exotica and education (1900s–1910s)
Conflict onstage
New system
Igorot shows tour the US
Vaudeville to bodabil
Laborers and performers (1920s–1930s)
Entertaining
Filipino American laborers onstage
Influences and consequences (1940s–1950s)
Filipino veterans onstage
American theater educators
English-language theater
America onstage
Babes on Broadway

2 Epiphanies (1960s–1970s)   *41*
Identity and awakenings
Filipino American and Asian American theater groups
Studying and establishing
East West Players in Los Angeles
Ating Tao in San Francisco
Dulaan ng mga Tao in Seattle
Endeavors in Hawaii
Grand Guignol in the Philippines
Philippine Educational Theatre Arts League in New York
Sining Bayan in Berkeley
Northwest Asian American Theatre in Seattle
Asian American Theater Company in San Francisco
Turned upside down
Pan Asian Repertory Theatre in New York
Philippine Martial Law onstage
Pilipino Cultural Night

3 Establish (1980s–1990s) *75*

Establishing more Filipino American theater groups
Filipino American theater educators
Writing plays
Spreading seeds
National Asian American Theatre Company in New York
Teatro ng Tanan in San Francisco
Ma-Yi Theater Company in New York
Backstage disciplines
CIRCA-Pintig in Chicago
The Filipino connection of "Miss Saigon"
Playwrights' Arena in Los Angeles
Writing more plays
Staging stories
Campo Santo in San Francisco
Creating characters
Endeavors in Washington, DC
Bindlestiff Studio in San Francisco

4 Engage (2000s–2010s) *125*

Developing and guiding
San Dionisio sa America in Los Angeles
Educating more students
Continuing against the odds
Coming together
Nurturing new works
Staging more stories
More playwrights
Directing and leading
Philippines onstage
Silver anniversaries
Continuing engagement

Acknowledgments *171*

References, readings, resources *173*

Index *179*

Introduction

Before the Philippines was colonized by Spain, natives of the archipelago termed their community-settlements as *barangay* (pronounced buh-rung-guy). Today, the term is still used to designate districts. Broadway, the theater district-industry in New York City, is a global icon for American theater. Aside from describing geography and communities, as used in this book's title, the terms "barangay" and "Broadway" serve to symbolize the Philippines and the United States of America, and the parts of their theater histories that are linked.

Though the Philippines had pre-colonial performance traditions and went on to adapt Western forms of theater from its Spanish colonizers, the trajectory of its theater development was sharply affected by American influence. The fabric of American theater, on the other hand, has always been enriched by foreign influence. It has been and continues to be woven with the participation of Filipinos—visiting, immigrant (by choice or circumstance), and US-born.

In less than 50 years after the US colonized the Philippines, at least one actor of Filipino heritage would already debut on a Broadway stage in a feature role. Throughout the US, there are many more stories of Filipino American theater before and after that milestone.

This book attempts to gather events and persons that have comprised Filipino American theater from 1898 to 2016: the performers of the 1900s and 1910s; the immigrant community productions of the 1920s and 1930s; the Broadway performers of the 1950s; the artists who were part of the seminal Filipino American theater groups and pioneering Asian American theater companies of the 1960s and 1970s; the Filipino American theater companies that were founded in the 1980s and 1990s; and the emerging theater makers of the 2000s and 2010s.

While the main vein of this book follows the different Filipino American theater groups that have been established throughout the decades, interviews with various theater makers provide insights to the pulse—both tribulations and triumphs—of their passion and vocation.

Their stories provide snapshots of the different barangay-communities that have been nurtured in, by, through, because of Filipino American theater—with barangay broadly drawn as the Filipino American community as a whole and intimately colored with sketches of individuals who have come together for the communities where they live, work, learn, teach, love, and perform.

*

The genesis for this book was sparked when, as part of my

journalism coverage of Filipino American theater, occasional searches for historical background information on individuals and groups yielded few readily-available resources.

Inspiration struck. From books such as Doreen Fernandez's "Palabas: Essays on Philippine Theater History," Lucy Mae San Pablo Burns' "Puro Arte: Filipinos on the Stages of Empire," and Esther Kim Lee's "A History of Asian American Theatre." And also from my previous research and writing work (as one of many contributors) for the Theater Volume of the forthcoming second edition of the Encyclopedia of Philippine Art (under editor-in-chief Nicanor Tiongson; published by the Cultural Center of the Philippines).

The strands of information found from these works further stoked my interest into a pressing drive to search for even more strands and to braid them together.

The result uses details and interviews—with theater makers such as directors, playwrights, designers, and actors—culled from my previously published articles in the newspaper Philippine Daily Inquirer and its online site Inquirer.net, combined with additional research and new interviews. My apologies for any shortcomings and inaccuracies.

Hopefully, this endeavor to provide an overview of its histories—while by no means a complete or definitive aggregation—will prove useful and fill an earnest step toward more and better documentation, journalism, reviews, research, studies, analyses, criticism, historiography, interpretations, and, ultimately, appreciation and enjoyment of Filipino American theater.

*

The Filipino word, spelling, and pronunciation for "Filipino" is "Pilipino." "Filipino" is used as gender-neutral in this book. In common use, some Filipino nouns are gendered, including "Filipina/o," "Pilipina/o," "Pinay/oy" (colloquial; from the last two syllables of "Filipina/o" appended by the letter Y) and "manang/ong" (an honorific for elders).

Filipino is based mostly on Tagalog, one of the most widely used out of more than a hundred languages in the Philippines. Organization names and production titles in Filipino are in Tagalog, unless noted otherwise. Aside from a few Filipino organizations and productions that have official English translations, most translations in this book are mine.

1
Entertainment
(1900s–1950s)

Exotica and education (1900s–1910s)

After three centuries as a Spanish colony, the Philippines declared its independence on June 12, 1898 with Emilio Aguinaldo as its first president.

The United States of America had declared war against Spain a few months earlier in April and the two countries had been battling it out in Cuba, another of Spain's colonies, and off the shores of Manila.

On August 13, the Philippines got a taste of theater that featured American players. The one-day performance of the Battle of Manila featured the Spanish armada fighting against and surrendering to the US squadron. The mock battle had been negotiated by the Spanish to avoid surrendering to the new Philippine government, thus preserving Spain's dignity.

American presence in the Philippines became the topic of theater productions in the US. Registered for copyright that year were Hilton Coon's "Under the American Flag," described as a "Spanish American drama in four acts" with Irish American and Spanish characters set in a garrison in Manila. There were also plays about the US squadron's earlier successful battle (led by Commodore George Dewey) against the Spanish armada in May such as Budd Randolph's "Dewey in Manila" and John Fraser's "Dewey, the hero of Manila," an "original naval drama in four acts."[1]

Meanwhile, the US had already begun having its share of Filipino performers. From June to October at the Trans-Mississippi and International Exposition in Omaha, Nebraska that year, there were "various men and women" at the Philippine Village located at the exposition's Streets of All Nations, "illustrating their customs, songs, language, habitations, avocations, etc."[2] And as the exposition drew to a close, a contingent of 16 "wild" Filipino "Manila warriors" arrived on October 26 to exhibit their war implements, customs, and dances.[3]

Spain lost its war with the US and, upon the signing of the Treaty of Paris on December 10, relinquished Cuba and

---

[1] Library of Congress Copyright Office. *Dramatic Compositions Copyrighted in the United States, 1870 to 1916. Volume 1, A-N*. Washington Government Printing Office. 1918.
[2] Hayes, James. *History of the Trans-Mississippi and International Exposition of 1898*. St. Louis: Woodward & Tiernam Printing Company. 1910.
[3] "Wild Filipinos to Be Exhibited at the Labyrinth." *Omaha World-Herald*. Oct. 26, 1898.

ceded its colonies Puerto Rico and Guam. With both countries ignoring the Philippines' declaration of independence, the deal included the archipelago. The Philippine government's resistance against American forces escalated into the Philippine-American War—or the Philippine insurrection, as US documents described it— starting on February 4, 1899.

The same fair organizers from Omaha went on to open the Greater America Exposition in 1899 (July–October) and recruited 35 Filipino performers. Theatrical press agent Pony Moore traveled to the Philippines to escort the contingent of "all kinds of actors" where "the entire lot are musicians," which included a woman who "does a magical act," an acrobat, and a harp soloist. Upon arriving in the US, he also recruited 18 of their ship's Filipino crew to perform at the fair.

The fair organizers had designed a Philippine Village with native huts, tropical plants, a lake, and even water buffalo. Throughout each day, the troupe dressed in white coats and trousers, sang American patriotic songs, danced American-style waltzes, and acted out what would have been their daily routines to unimpressed fairgoers who did not find them exotic enough.[4]

Aguinaldo was captured by American forces on March 23, 1901. US president William McKinley appointed William Howard Taft as the Philippines' governor, establishing the American colonial government. Moore returned to Manila

---

[4] Hawkins, Michael. "Undecided Empire: The Travails of Imperial Representation of Filipinos at the Greater America Exposition, 1899." *Philippine Studies*, Vol. 63, No. 3, 2015. Quezon City: Ateneo de Manila University.

that year to recruit 100 Filipinos, this time for the Pan-American Exposition in Buffalo, New York (May–November). In an 11-acre enclosure, they performed daily routines such as washing clothes, riding a water buffalo, and holding cockfights.[5]

Conflict onstage

Prior to Spanish colonization, the natives (comprised of different ethnolinguistic groups) of the islands that would become known as the Philippines had their own performance forms and traditions such as songs and dances embedded in rituals, ceremonies, and other customs. Under Spanish rule, Filipinos eventually began using and localizing theater forms and genres from Spain such as prose or verse plays called *drama.*

There was also the *sarsuwela* (previous spellings include *sarswela* and *sarsuela*), a type of musical theater adapted from the Spanish *zarzuela* (itself adapted from Italian operettas), with stories usually featuring lovers of different social status overcoming odds for a happy ending.

In November 1901, the American colonial government passed the Sedition Act in the Philippines, making any form of advocating for independence a crime. Nonetheless, Filipino theater makers staged works that contained messages against American occupation for which they were raided, arrested, tried, and imprisoned. Filipino theater scholars would later describe these playwrights' allegorical

---

[5] Hartt, Mary Bronson. "How to See the Pan-American Exposition." Sept. 12, 1901. Doing the Pan website: Panam1901.org. https://panam1901.org/documents/howtosee.htm

works as *drama simbolico* [symbolic drama] or *drama politikal* [political drama].

Examples include Juan Abad's "Tanikalang Guinto" ["Golden Chain"] in 1902 and Aurelio Tolentino's "Kahapon, Ngayon at Bukas" ["Yesterday, Today and Tomorrow"] in 1904, among others. Characters had names such as Dalita [Misery] and Karangalan [Honor], props included flags with revolutionary emblems, and costumes were color-coded so that actors could form representations of the Philippine flag, which was prohibited from being publicly displayed.

Arthur Stanley Riggs (1879–1952) served in the US Naval Auxiliary Force during the war and lived in the Philippines from 1902 to 1904. He followed the "seditious plays," as they were later collectively labeled, watching performances and attending court sessions. In 1905, he wrote the book "Filipino Drama," which details the productions he had witnessed and includes English translations of six plays.

In the years leading up to and during its occupation by America, the Philippines became the subject matter or setting for theater productions in the US, such as Charles Blaney's romance adventure "Across the Pacific" (1900), about an American soldier who joins the Philippine-American War; and Clyde Fitch's play, "Her Own Way" (1903), where an American woman's beau is deployed to the Philippines to fight against insurrections.

George Ade's comic opera "Sultan of Sulu" (1902) is about American soldiers interrupting a Filipino sultan's search for a new spouse. Ade disagreed with US colonization of the Philippines and wrote his opera to mock the proceedings and legislations. "Sultan" was staged in Chicago, Boston, and New York, and toured large cities for three years, establishing Ade's reputation as a musical comedy writer.[6]

The 1907 musical comedy "Shoo Fly Regiment," by African Americans Bob Cole (book) and John Rosamond Johnson (music), is about how a black soldier's relationship with his fiancee is interrupted when he volunteers to fight in the Philippine-American War. The show's cast of characters includes "A Filipino spy" (unnamed) and Grizelle, "a Filipino dancer." It includes songs such as "On the Gay Luneta," referencing Luneta Park in Manila, and "Down in the Philippines." The production toured several states, which included a run in New York City at the Grand Opera House and Bijou Theater.

In 1915, Jerome Kern (music), Harry Smith (lyrics), and Guy Bolton (book) created the musical comedy "90 in the Shade," where an American woman who travels to the Philippines to meet her fiance (who is working there) ends up with two additional suitors, one American and the other, an "educated Filipino" named Mozi.

The Filipino characters in "Sultan of Sulu" (the Sultan and his spouses), "Shoo Fly Regiment" (the spy and Grizelle), and "90 in the Shade" (Mozi) were not played by Filipino actors.

There are also other plays, operettas, and burlesques with "Manila" or "Philippines" in their titles or descriptions that

---

[6] Fulton, Robert. "George Ade's Comic Opera The Sultan of Sulu 1902." Moroland History website: Morolandhistory.com. 2007.
http://morolandhistory.com/Related%20Articles/Ade%27s%20Sultan%20of%20Sulu.htm

are listed—more than 20 entries—in the publication "Dramatic Compositions Copyrighted in the United States, 1870 to 1916."

New system

The colonial government established a new education system in the Philippines that used English as the language of instruction.

It also passed the Pensionado Act in 1903, which granted scholarships to Filipinos from affluent and influential families to study at colleges or universities in America in exchange for public service upon their return. ["Pension" is Spanish for "financial aid;" "pensionado" is "pensioner."]

The education system introduced drama forms in English, though the first playwright in English to be taught was not an American one. In 1904, David Barrows, the general superintendent for education, included William Shakespeare's "Julius Caesar" and "The Merchant of Venice" in the curriculum for high school juniors.[7]

Shakespeare was not entirely unfamiliar to Filipinos as there was already GD Roke's "Ang Sintang Dalisay ni Julieta at Romeo" ["The Pure Love of Julieta and Romeo"], a 1901 Tagalog metrical poem adaptation of "Romeo and Juliet." This mandate, however, would have created wider exposure to the Bard's works in his original tongue.

---

[7] Ick, Judy Celine. "Ilonggos, Igorottes, Merchants, and Jews: Shakespeare and American Colonial Education in the Philippines." Patajo-Legasto, Priscelina; ed. *Philippine Studies: Have We Gone Beyond St. Louis?* Quezon City: University of the Philippines Press. 2008.

By 1915, the first play in English by Filipinos would be written: Jesusa Araullo and Lino Castillejo's "A Modern Filipina." The plot features an independent young woman who plays along with her suitor's faked tree-fall injury—his attempt to appeal to her sympathies—since she liked him anyway.

Igorot shows tour the US

Though Filipinos had already performed three separate times in the US at the world's fairs in Omaha and Buffalo, those were just a lead-up to a much larger performance.

In 1904, the colonial government sent more than a thousand Filipinos to St. Louis, Missouri to perform at the Louisiana Purchase Exposition, also known as the 1904 World's Fair or the St. Louis World's Fair.

The contingent included the Philippine Constabulary and its band, Boy Scouts, midget siblings Martina and Juan de la Cruz (who were later reportedly signed up by the Barnum and Bailey Circus[8]), as well as several groups of indigenous peoples. Pensionado students were assigned to work as ushers for fairgoers before being deployed to their schools.

Also included in the contingent were the Igorot (also spelled Igorrote in documents from that time), a blanket term for indigenous peoples from the northern highlands which include the Bontoc.

---

[8] Silva, John. "Little Brown Brothers' St. Louis Blues: The Philippine Exposition, 1904 St. Louis World's Fair." Positively Filipino website: Positivelyfilipino.com. June 5, 2013.
http://positivelyfilipino.com/magazine/2013/6/little-brown-brothers-st-louis-blues-the-philippine-exposition-1904-st-louis-worlds-fair

The Philippine Reservation was the major component of the fair, taking up 47 of the 82 acres allotted for exhibitions. Though there were more than 40 different exhibitions at the reservation, the Igorot exhibition was the hit show. With their scantily clad and tattooed bodies, the Igorot performed dances to gong music at scheduled times during the day. They also staged demonstrations of blacksmithing, metalworking, and weaving.

One of the Bontoc, Antero Cabrera (who later dropped the surname of his adoptive Ilocano parents), was popular with the press for his ability to sing American songs. He had learned English from working with American anthropologists and missionaries to the Philippines and was even the designated translator for the Igorot delegation's visit to the White House.

But what really drew the crowds were the daily performances of dog eating, something that was not an actual daily practice of the Igorot—as they only did so occasionally for ceremonial purposes. For the fair's April to December run, the number of attendees was estimated at 19 million. Filipinos were displayed alongside Native American peoples, Africans, dwarves, and bearded ladies.[9]

The following year, new groups of Bontoc, including some who had been to St. Louis, entered into contracts with two veterans of the Spanish-American War who wanted to tour their respective Igorot shows in the US. Truman Hunt's Igorot Exhibit Company (which lasted a year) and Richard

---

[9] Afable, Patricia. "Journeys from Bontoc to the Western Fairs, 1904-1915: The 'Nikimalika' and their Interpreters." *Philippine Studies*, Vol. 52, No. 4, 2004. Quezon City: Ateneo de Manila University.

Schneidewind's Filipino Exhibition Company went on to exhibit the Bontoc in expositions, amusement parks, and county fairs across the US until 1914, when the colonial government in the Philippines banned the practice.

By then, over 200 Bontoc men and women had performed in Igorot shows in cities such as New York, Chicago, Los Angeles, and San Francisco, as well as at world's fairs like the 1905 Lewis and Clark Centennial Exposition in Portland, Oregon, the 1907 Jamestown Exposition in Hampton Roads, Virginia, and the 1909 Alaska-Yukon Pacific Exposition in Seattle, Washington, among others.

In 1906, Filipino students attending University of California-Berkeley led a protest against the Igorot show that was on its way to the Jamestown Exposition.[10] Decades later, this would be mirrored by Filipino Americans and other Asian Americans protesting "Miss Saigon," a musical that opened on Broadway in 1991 (and starred a Filipino actor in one of the lead roles), for its negative stereotypes of Asians.

Vaudeville to bodabil

During the 1900s in America, silent motion pictures started becoming available through nickelodeons. Popular music genres included blues and ragtime; jazz was starting to be noticed. Electricity started becoming commercially available, with New York City's Broadway being one of the

---

[10] Elinson, Elaine. "Igorots Arrive in San Francisco in 1905." Found SF website: FoundSF.org. Undated.
http://foundsf.org/index.php?title=Igorots_Arrive_in_San_Francisco_in_1905

first streets to be lit with marquees that had white light bulbs, earning it the nickname The Great White Way.

Outside New York City, community theaters and stock theater companies (theaters with a resident pool of actors performing a repertory of stock productions) competed with touring companies (groups that performed across the country in theaters usually owned by the Theatrical Syndicate). The Syndicate was a group of theater owners that consolidated ticket sales and monopolized touring theater companies by booking them on assigned routes and schedules for its own network of theaters.

Though by the end of the 1910s, most of the theaters on Broadway and much of the US would be taken over by the Shubert Organization (founded by the Shubert siblings Sam, Lee, and Jacob; children of Jewish immigrants from Russia) and the Nederlander Organization (founded by David Nederlander). Theater owners and producers were not the only ones who consolidated their reach. In 1913, more than a hundred professional actors in New York City banded together to establish Actors' Equity Association, the labor union for actors performing in live theatrical productions.

As a reaction to the commercialism of the Broadway industry, the Little Theater movement of the 1910s and 1920s nurtured works by new playwrights that were staged by small theater troupes. It was also during this time when acting and staging styles transitioned from declamatory to naturalistic, as influenced by the works of French, German, and Russian theater artists such as Andre Antoine, Otto Brahm, and Konstantin Stanislavski, among others.

While touring shows from Europe and Broadway productions such as plays, musicals, opera, symphonies, and revues (shows that combine music, sketches, dance, and chorus girls—the most popular of which was the Ziegfeld Follies) were available to those who could afford it in New York, other forms of live entertainment for most Americans in the 1900s included minstrel shows (where white actors wear blackface make up and lampoon African Americans) and vaudeville shows (programs that include a mix of skits and acts by comics, magicians, and ventriloquists, and even acts with animals). Vaudeville rose in popularity in the 1900s and would peak in the 1910s.

In 1915, Luis Borromeo (1879–1945), a native of Leyte province, traveled to San Francisco to attend the Panama-Pacific International Exposition. His piano-playing skills were discovered and he went on to perform for several years on the Orpheum circuit, a chain of vaudeville theaters. He returned to the Philippines in 1921, renamed himself Borromeo Lou, and became an impresario of localized jazz and vaudeville shows, helping to popularize a new form of entertainment in the country. He termed his shows *vod-a-vil*, which became known as *bodabil* in the vernacular.

Laborers and performers (1920s–1930s)

The optimism that followed World War I (1914–1918) gave rise to the affluent Roaring Twenties. The production and sales of alcoholic beverages were banned during the Prohibition Era (1920–1933), causing saloons to be replaced by speakeasies. It was at these speakeasies where jazz music blossomed. Radio became popular and television was in its nascent form. Silent films gave way to talkies (film with sound).

During the Great Depression (1929–1939), a period of economic downturn that left many without jobs, the Federal Theatre Project was established by the government as a relief measure to employ theater artists and workers by funding performances across the US. Headed by theater artist Hallie Flanagan, the project lasted from 1935 to 1939.

Filipinos had been traveling to the North American continent centuries before the US declared independence in 1776. Some Filipinos journeyed aboard galleons from Manila and landed on California as early as the 1580s. (Still unclaimed at the time, California would be claimed by Spain in 1769 and ceded to the US in 1848.) There were also some Filipinos who settled in Louisiana as early as the 1760s. (Owned by Spain at the time, Louisiana would be purchased by the US from France in 1803.)

A series of previous US government legislation helped allow a wave of Filipino immigration to occur in the 1920s and 1930s to fill labor shortages in the agriculture and fishing industries.

Chinese laborers recruited to work on the transcontinental railroad spurred the passage of the 1875 Page Act and the 1882 Chinese Exclusion Act, both of which blocked immigration from China. Japanese workers who replaced the Chinese spurred the 1907 Gentlemen's Agreement, which prohibited the entry of immigrants from Japan. The 1917 Asiatic Barred Zone Act and the 1924 Asian Exclusion Act further hindered immigrants from Asia.

But because the Philippines was an American colony, Filipinos were categorized as nationals and not as aliens, and could freely enter the US. Filipino men continued to move to Hawaii to work at the sugar plantations, which they had started doing so as early as 1906, and started to move to Alaska to work at fish canneries and to the West Coast to harvest crops at farms. To support themselves, Filipinos who traveled to the US for education without scholarships would also work as farm laborers or in service occupations such as waiters, cooks, barbers, bellboys, janitors, etc.

As encountered by the other waves of Asian immigrants to the US, discrimination was also experienced by Filipinos. Public venues such as restaurants, hotels, and cinemas had signs that read "Positively No Filipinos Allowed" or "No Dogs And Filipinos Allowed." In California, anti-Filipino riots broke out in Exeter in 1929 and in Watsonville in 1930, among other places.

A few years later, provisions in the 1934 Tydings-McDuffie Act reclassified Filipinos from nationals to aliens—by making the Philippines a commonwealth of the US—and imposed an annual quota on immigrants from the Philippines (which is why it is also known as the Filipino Exclusion Act).

Entertaining

The growing number of Filipino immigrants in America created pockets of communities that provided performers and audiences for amateur and community theater productions.

Filipino Catholic Club Drama Guild in Seattle

At 21 years old, Baltazar "Bob" Fernandez Flor immigrated in 1921 to the US from Guimbal, Iloilo province to take up a bachelor's degree in education at Seattle College. To support himself, he wrote for several Filipino American newspapers and also worked as a cook for the US Coast and Geodetic Survey.

In the 1930s, he established the Filipino Catholic Club Drama Guild and wrote plays. His works were staged at Maryknoll Hall, a church exclusively for Japanese and Filipinos. Information about Flor's work as a playwright was brought to light in 2003 when his younger brother's son, Robert Francis Fernandez Flor (1943–), unearthed his personal effects and discovered "love letters from several women and a few from a scolding priest, programs from plays he'd written, and one surviving play."[11]

The extant work is "Retribution," a play set in the Philippines that centers around Juan and his attempt to avenge his father's death, though matters are complicated when the offending party turns out to be his beloved's father. There is also a surviving playbill for a Jan. 7, 1940 performance of "The Eve of the Fiesta of St. Vincent de Ferrer," though no synopsis is provided. Both documents list Baltazar's pen name "Bob Flor" as the playwright.

"Unfortunately, Baltazar suffered a heart attack in the summer of 1940 in Cordova, Alaska, while working aboard the SS Surveyor," said Robert, who was born in Seattle and

---

[11] Ang, Walter. "Anti-beauty pageant Fil-Am teens to be depicted on stage." *Inquirer.net.* Sept. 7, 2017. http://usa.inquirer.net/6537/anti-beauty-pageant-fil-teens-depicted-stage

would go on to be inspired by his uncle's works and become a playwright himself in the 2010s. Robert had shown his uncle's effects to his friends and they suggested that the materials could be fashioned into a play. "Not knowing how to write one, I enrolled in courses at A Contemporary Theatre (ACT), Freehold, and Seattle Repertory theaters," he said. Scenes from his "My Uncle's Letters" were performed in ACT's Multicultural Playwrights Festival in 2014. Robert has continued to write plays since.

Also found among Baltazar's effects was a one-act play by Trinidad Rojo (1902–94) titled "Lights Off and a Double Surprise." Presumed to have also been written in the 1930s, the play is about two Filipino fish cannery workers in Alaska and their love interests. Rojo moved from the Philippines to Seattle in 1926, attending University of Washington while working as a laborer. He graduated in 1930 with a bachelor's degree in English, comparative literature, and drama; and went on to become a poet and civic leader.

Filipino Art Lovers Club in Honolulu

Rafaela Pandaraoan Valentin (1896–1991), originally from Piddig, Ilocos Norte province, moved to the American territory of Hawaii in 1926 (it would not become a state until 1959). She taught folk dance to Filipino children at the International Institute of the YWCA (Young Women's Christian Association) and later at Pohukaina School and University of Hawaii, while her spouse Juan worked as an accountant for the Hawaiian Sugar Planters Association.[12]

---

[12] Cooke, Mary. "Fifty years of devotion to Filipino cultural arts." *The Honolulu Advertiser*. Oct. 12, 1976.

In 1932, she founded a troupe that would perform at community events and, in 1939, she staged an Ilocano sarsuwela. In 1940, she founded the Filipino Art Lovers Club, training its members in performing, and directing its programs. The club's principal dancers were Valentin's son Orlando and his spouse Priscilla, both of whom would go on to found Pearl of the Orient Dance Company in 1960.

Through the club, Valentin established the Punahou Music School scholarship for Filipino students studying for musical careers. Other productions staged by the club include "Pantomima de Amor" ["Love Pantomime"], which Valentin wrote and directed. In 1956, she sponsored the founding of the Philippine Veterans' Band, composed of Filipino musicians who had retired from armed services bands and the Royal Hawaiian Band.

There were other Filipino performers who settled in Hawaii. Andres Baclig, who had been a big band clarinet player in Manila, opted to stay in Hawaii in 1926 when he toured there with his band, the Manila Synchopators. He and his spouse Lucille went on to lead the Royal Serenaders band. Baclig's bandmate Gabe Baltazar went on to play clarinet with the Royal Hawaiian Band.

Even earlier, in 1888, traveling musicians Jose Lebornio, Francisco de los Santos, Geronimo Inocencio, and Lazaro Salamanca all ended up joining the Royal Hawaiian Band when they decided to stay in Hawaii while en route to the United States.[13]

---

[13] Dionisio, Juan; executive ed. *The Filipinos in Hawaii......The First 75 Years 1906-1981*. Hawaii Filipino News Specialty Publications. 1981.

Love Eternal in Stockton

Lucia "Lucing" Funcion Cordova, originally from Aklan province, moved to Stockton, California in 1929 and taught Tagalog language classes. She wrote and directed the sarsuwela "Walang Kamatayang Pagibig" ["Love Eternal"] for Stockton's first annual Filipino Carnival in 1937. Playing the lead roles were Sally Accompanado and Raymundo Cruz.[14]

Serenaders in the West Coast

Born in La Union province, Francisco "Frank" Osias (1909–2003) traveled to the US in 1928, hoping to enter medical school. He ended up meeting Filipino members of the band Moonlight Serenaders and learned to play the alto saxophone. Osias went on the road with the band for seven years, touring the West Coast, then as far east as Missouri and as far south as Texas. He was still a working musician until his early 70s, playing with several other bands in Seattle.[15] Carlos Malla, who was based in Seattle, joined the 18-piece orchestra Manila Serenaders in 1934. The group, which later changed its name to Manila Swingsters, also toured across the US.[16]

Filipino singers, dancers, and musicians also performed at Chinese nightclubs in San Francisco, such as Chinese Sky Room (opened in 1936) and Forbidden City (opened in 1938). Japanese, Korean, and Filipino entertainers would change their names to pass for Chinese, including Arlene and Tony Wing, siblings whose real names were Arlene and

---

[14] Cordova, Fred. *Filipinos: Forgotten Asian Americans, A Pictorial Essay 1763–Circa 1963*. Dubuque: Kendall/Hunt Publishing Company. 1983.
[15] "Obituary: Frank L. (Francisco) Osias." *The Seattle Times*. Oct. 9, 2003.
[16] Cordova.

Gonzalo Anthony Lagrimas.[17] Tony went on to perform at nightclubs well into the 1960s. He also taught dance and even ran his own studio. In the late 1940s to early 1950s, Filipino bodabil and jazz singer Katy de la Cruz (whose real name is Catalina) was a top-billed performer at Forbidden City.

Filipino Americans "portraying" Chinese Americans in a Chinese nightclub in San Francisco would be mirrored a few decades later on the opposite coast in 1958, when Filipino Americans are cast as Chinese American characters in "Flower Drum Song," a Broadway musical inspired by these nightclubs.

Filipino American laborers onstage

The lives of and situations faced by immigrant Filipino laborers have been tackled onstage.

Carlos Bulosan

Carlos Bulosan immigrated to Alaska in 1930. After initially working in farms and in other service occupations, he eventually became a writer. He detailed the frustrations and indignities of being an immigrant laborer in short stories like "The Romance of Magno Rubio" and in his semi-autobiographical 1946 novel "America is in the Heart."

Bulosan's life and works have inspired numerous stage adaptations. Some examples include Stan Asis' adaptation of Bulosan's works into "Philippine Legends, Folklore and American Impressions" for Theatrical Ensemble of Asians

---

[17] Filipino American National Historical Society, et al. *Filipinos in San Francisco*. Charleston: Arcadia Publishing. 2011.

(later renamed Northwest Asian American Theatre) in Seattle (1975); Chris Millado's adaptation of "America is in the Heart" for Pintig Cultural Group in Chicago (1992); and Giovanni Ortega's play about Bulosan's life in "Allos, the story of Carlos Bulosan" for East West Players in Los Angeles (2011).

Romance of Magno Rubio

"The Romance of Magno Rubio" has been adapted for the stage by Nancy Rebusit in 1984 for Northwest Asian American Theatre and by Lonnie Carter in 2002 for Ma-Yi Theater in New York. Carter's version features Magno, "a short Filipino migrant worker who longs for love" in the central valleys of California in the 1930s. Magno goes on to have a long-distance relationship through love letters with his pen pal Clarabelle from Arkansas but soon realizes "reality and dreams do not always align."

1965 Grape Strike

"Welga," a play by Conrad Panganiban, features a teenager inspired by union leader Larry Itliong's life story to become more aware of his and his mother's rights ["Welga" means "strike"]. "I knew about the manong through having to read the novel 'America is in the Heart,'" Panganiban said.[18] ["Manong" is an honorific for older men, as well as for the immigrant laborers of the 1920s and 1930s.]

The play has received developmental staged readings in San Francisco by groups such as Bindlestiff Studio and will be staged in a full production in 2017.

---

[18] Ang, Walter. "Play inspired by labor leader Larry Itliong to premiere in SF." *Inquirer.net*. Sept. 22, 2017. http://usa.inquirer.net/6852/play-inspired-labor-leader-larry-itliong-premiere-sf

Itliong immigrated to the US in 1929, became a union leader, and together with other Filipino organizers like Philip Vera Cruz, led the 1965 Grape Strike in Delano, California. Itliong was instrumental in convincing the Mexican laborers, led by Cesar Chavez, not to replace and fill the vacated jobs of the striking Filipino workers but to join the strike instead. The strike lasted for five years and led to a breakthrough in labor rights in the US.

1977 International Hotel Eviction
American Conservatory Theater in San Francisco staged "Monstress" in 2015, a twin bill of one-acts adapted from short-story writer Lysley Tenorio's works. Sean San Jose adapted "Presenting ... The Monstress!" and Japanese American Philip Kan Gotanda adapted "Remember the I-Hotel."

The latter play features the relationship between two Filipino immigrant laborers over many years, ending with their eviction from the titular hotel. The story of "Remember the I-Hotel" was inspired by the 1977 eviction of Filipino and Chinese tenants from the International Hotel in San Francisco's former Manilatown section. Due to existing laws upon and subsequently after their arrival, Filipino immigrants were not allowed to marry white Americans nor to own land and businesses.

Some of the men grew into old age as bachelors with low incomes and meager Social Security benefits in their retirement, residing in working-class single-room-occupancy hotels such as the International Hotel. As the elderly men had no families and nowhere else to go, the eviction drew protests but was not stopped.

Influences and consequences (1940s-1950s)

The 1934 Tydings-McDuffie Act allowed for the Philippines to become an independent country, subject to a 10-year transition period as a commonwealth of the US (which is why it is also known as the Philippine Independence Act). The last few years of the transition were interrupted by World War II.

In December 1941, Japanese forces bombed Pearl Harbor in Hawaii and launched air raids on US military installations in the Philippines. Recruitment of Filipinos into the United States Armed Forces in the Far East (USAFFE) had already begun earlier that year. In the US, Filipino Americans who enlisted in the Army were formed into the First and Second Filipino Infantry Regiments in 1942.

The Philippines was occupied by Japan from 1942 to 1945. After it was liberated by Filipino and American forces in 1945, the Philippines became an independent country again upon the signing of the 1946 Treaty of Manila.

The 1946 Luce-Celler Act restricted immigrants from the Philippines to the US to only a hundred a year. However, other channels of immigration continued via the 1945 War Brides Act (which exempted alien spouses and children of members of the US Armed Forces from immigrant quotas) and from the US Navy's granting of naturalization benefits to enlisted Filipinos. Filipinos have been recruited to join the Navy since 1901, with enlistment continuing until 1992, when the US withdrew from its leased military air and naval bases in the Philippines.

Starting in 1948, the Exchange Visitor Program provided

Filipino nurses, mostly women at the time, the opportunity to train in the US—which led to opportunities to be recruited for employment to fill staffing shortages. Nurses from the Philippines were preferred candidates partly because of their familiarity with the English language and American standards of healthcare since nursing education in the Philippines had been patterned after American models.

Filipino veterans onstage

Unlike the Filipinos who joined the Navy and the Filipino Americans who enlisted in the Army in the US, Filipinos who enlisted with the USAFFE were denied initial offers of American citizenship and full veterans' benefits—which were reneged under the 1946 Rescission Act. After the act was retracted in 1990, citizenship was granted to those who were able to avail of it, though benefits were still denied. In 2009, lump sums were paid out to surviving veterans.

Bindlestiff Studio staged Filipino playwright Rodolfo "Rody" Vera's "The Guerrillas of Powell Street" in 2014. Adapted from Benjamin Pimentel's novel "Mga Gerilya Sa Powell Street," the play features fictitious Filipino WWII veterans in San Francisco as they reminisce about their days in the war and ruminate their mortality.

Pimentel moved to the US in 1990 and took graduate studies in journalism at University of California-Berkeley. "It was the same time when Filipino veterans started moving to the area after they were finally given the opportunity to become American citizens," he said. However, they were still denied regular benefits and were only receiving supplemental security income, roughly $600. "They need to survive on less than that in order to send home money to their families, which, in San Francisco, is virtually impossible."

Pimentel found out that the men—in order to save money—would share one room, with up to 10 people per room, and would eat at soup kitchens. He had noticed the veterans staying by one of the train stations on Powell Street. "Many of these men were old and sick. San Francisco can be a beautiful place, but the weather can be brutal," he said.

The veterans were waiting for the passage of an Equity Bill that would grant them equal benefits as other American WWII veterans. However, if they were to die before the bill's passage, funds would be insufficient to repatriate their bodies. "For many Filipinos, cremation is a 'no, no,'" he said. Their plight formed the premise for the play: men who are fighting cold, hunger, and loneliness while waiting for their benefits and for their "long-distance call from heaven."[19]

In his column for Inquirer.net, Pimentel wrote about an incident after the show had closed. As the Bindlestiff staff were cleaning up on a Sunday afternoon, recently widowed veteran Francisco Viray stepped in to ask about the show. Producer Lorna Velasco described the incident as "an unforgettable moment" and what had transpired as being on top of her "list of great experiences in theater."

"All our faces were crestfallen, as we told him regrettably that last night was the last show," Lorna

---

[19] Ang. "A writer's sense of mission." *Philippine Daily Inquirer (PDI)*. Nov. 24, 2008.

continued. But for a community theater group based in a tough neighborhood where its members dream of using theater to tell stories of people whose stories are typically forgotten, one can always improvise.

"Without missing a beat, [producer] Joyce Juan, [actors] Rhoda Gravador and Joshua Icban offered to sing and play for him. I jumped down the stairs to gather [actors] Michael Dorado and Allan Manalo to see if they too would like to sing for him. For half an hour, we went through all the songs from the play. Manong Francisco clapped, laughed and sang along.

"We just about lost it when Manong Francisco sang every word from the Green Beret song (Major Amor) along with us," she recalled. That's the Tagalog version of the Hollywood movie tune that one of the play's main characters, Major Rodolfo Amor, sang after his death.

"For the rest of the hour, he shared stories of his time in the war, his wife who recently passed and, as a token of his gratitude, recited an eloquent deep Tagalog poem for us. It summed up, in an unexpected way, what this show has meant to all of us," she said.

Pimentel wrote that the incident also "summed what Bindlestiff has come to mean to community theater and to many Filipinos in San Francisco."[20]

---

[20] Pimentel, Benjamin. "Oddly named Fil-Am theater group with a big heart." *Inquirer.net*. Aug. 7, 2014. http://globalnation.inquirer.net/109049/oddly-named-fil-am-theater-group-with-a-big-heart (Excerpts used with permission.)

American theater educators

Educators who taught American ways of making theater to Filipino students included Jesuit priest Henry Lee Irwin (1892–1976), who moved to Manila and taught English dramatics to college and high school students at Ateneo de Manila (later University). Born in Bridgeport, Connecticut, Irwin had acted with a stock theater group in his youth.[21] In the early 1920s, he directed plays such as "Julius Caesar" and "Damon and Pythias" for the school's theater group, the Ateneo Players' Guild.

Born in New Jersey, James Bertram Reuter (1916-2012) was another Jesuit priest who first arrived in the Philippines in 1938. During WWII, Reuter and Irwin were placed in an internment camp by the Japanese army. After the war, both returned to the US briefly.

Irwin returned to Manila to continue teaching and directing productions, even with a 1950 production amidst Ateneo's post-war ruins. An advocate of Shakespeare's works, he directed them with student casts throughout his career. Ateneo went on to name its 1,131-seat theater after him.

During his time back in the US, Reuter studied radio and television communications at Fordham University, New York. In 1948, he returned to Manila and taught at Ateneo and Saint Paul College (later University). He trained students in singing and acting; he also directed theater productions "from Rodgers and Hammerstein to Cole Porter and Gilbert and Sullivan."[22] Reuter became a well-known

---

[21] Ordoñez, Minyong. "Jesuits who brought life to our theater arts." *PDI*. Sept. 14, 2014.
[22] Cruz, Isagani. "Good-bye Father Reuter." *The Philippine Star*. Jan. 10, 2013.

public figure for his writing and directing work in theater, radio, television, and film. Saint Paul University named its theater after him, and, in 1984, the government named him an honorary Filipino citizen.

Minnesota-native Jean Garrot-Edades (1907–97) taught English and drama at University of the Philippines (UP). Garrot was studying at University of Washington (UW) in Seattle when she met her future spouse Victorio Edades. She moved to Manila with him in 1928 and became one of the first directors of the UP Dramatic Club by 1930. Victorio, who had gone to UW to study architecture and then a master's in painting, designed the sets for her productions.

Garrot-Edades was repatriated to the US after WWII, during which she studied for a master's in theater arts at University of Chicago's Godwin Theatre School. She returned to the Philippines after two years and resumed teaching as well as producing and directing plays.

In the late 1950s, she edited the anthologies "Short Plays of the Philippines, including Advice for the amateur director" and "More Short Plays of the Philippines."

In the late 1960s, she relocated to Davao City with her spouse, where she founded the theater group Philippine Theatre Davao. She also wrote "Onstage and Offstage" (1983), a memoir of her theater work that also includes six one-act plays in English written by her former students.

*

The education of Filipino theater artists in the US was another contributing aspect of how their philosophies for theater making would follow ongoing American methods, models, and ideals.

Opportunities for exchange studies were aided by scholarship organizations such as the Fulbright Program (founded by senator James William Fulbright and funded by the US Bureau of Educational and Cultural Affairs) and by philanthropic organizations such as the Rockefeller Foundation (established by industrialist John Davison Rockefeller).

Severino Montano (1915–80) was one scholar from this era who went on to become an influential playwright (in English) and director in the Philippines from the 1950s to the 1960s. He had studied drama at UP (Garrot-Edades was one of his teachers) before pursuing a master's degree in playwriting and production at Yale University on scholarship, which he completed in 1942. He spent the war years working for the Philippine government-in-exile in the US. Upon his return to Manila in 1953, he founded Arena Theater, which staged his plays in Manila and the provinces.

English-language theater

The American education system that was established in the Philippines in 1901 had instilled and perpetuated English usage to a point where, by the 1930s, it had become "the language of the educated, the intelligentsia, and the elite," wrote theater scholar Doreen Fernandez in her book "Palabas: Essays on Philippine Theater History."

She further noted that theater forms and genres in

vernacular languages were soon deemed fit only for rural areas and for the unschooled. All the while, Filipinos continued to be exposed to American forms and styles of entertainment like Hollywood musical films, theatrical revues, and vaudeville shows.

After WWII, school, amateur, and professional theater groups in Manila resumed staging productions in English by American and British playwrights, including European works in English translations.

One such amateur group even included American members. Manila Theatre Guild, which was composed of American and British expatriates, staged Broadway musicals and plays from the late 1940s onward. Among its members was David Harvey McTurk, who had moved to Manila in the late 1930s after previously working as a nightclub entertainer in Shanghai. During WWII, he put on shows at the prison camp where he was interned. With the stage name Dave Harvey, he acted in and directed shows for the guild.[23]

While there were theater groups that continued to stage material in vernacular languages, English was so entrenched in society that a tally of productions staged in Manila from 1946 to 1964 showed 879 in English (567 foreign, 312 by local playwrights) to only 66 in Filipino (out of which 26 were translations of foreign plays).[24]

---

[23] Gopal, Lou. "The Army Navy Club Manila Nostalgia." Manila Nostalgia website: LouGopal.com/Manila. Sept. 16, 2014.
http://lougopal.com/manila/?p=2370
[24] Legasto-Patajo, Priscelina. "Wow! These Americans." in *Philippine Studies: Have We Gone Beyond St. Louis?*

Renewed and sustained interest in and creation of Filipino theater productions in local languages would only start to take root in the mid- to late-1960s at the beginnings of a nationalist wave.

Filipino theater scholars have noted the wide reach of American influence on Philippine theater that lasted well into the 1950s. Fernandez wrote, "The idea of theatre, its form and content, and its social function of education and entertainment were thus, for the schooled Filipinos of the first half of the twentieth century, shaped according to the American model."[25]

America onstage

The complicated relationship between the Philippines and America has served as a source of subject matter for theater work in the Philippines.

After World War II

After WWII, some Filipino playwrights used humor to criticize prevailing attitudes toward America. Wilfrido Guerrero wrote "Wow! These Americans" (1947), a one-act comedy about two American soldiers who visit a solicitous Filipino family, where one sibling ends up killing a villainous Japanese captain by accident. The play was popular after the war for its satire of Filipinos' colonial mentality (i.e. the belief in the superiority of colonizers).[26]

---

[25] Fernandez, Doreen. *Palabas: Essays on Philippine Theater History*. Quezon City: Ateneo de Manila University Press. 1996.

[26] Martinez, Maria Carmela. "An Annotated Bibliography of the Theatrical Performances of Wilfrido Ma. Guerrero's Plays." Undergraduate thesis at De La Salle University-Manila. 2004.

Severino Montano's one-act satire "The Ladies and the Senator" (1953) is about the members of the Filipino Women's Club in Washington, DC who gossip about their politician spouses' corruption and shady affairs. Marcelino Agana's "New Yorker in Tondo" (1954) is a one-act comedy about Kikay, who returns to the Tondo district of Manila after living in New York, where her newfound affectations of an urban American bewilder her mother and friends.

There were also works that sought to dramatize negative consequences of communing with colonizers. Montano's one-act "Sabina" (1953) features a Filipino country lass who falls in love with an American businessman who turns out to be already married. The revelation causes Sabina, pregnant by then, to shoot herself.

Later works

Later decades would have more straightforward and pointed material or directorial stances in their commentary of American influence in the Philippines.

Some examples include Philippine Educational Theater Association (PETA)'s 1967 staging of "Bayaning Huwad," a translation of Virginia Moreno's "Straw Patriot," a play about a farmer who sells his daughter to an American soldier. In 1991, PETA staged "Minsa'y Isang Gamu-gamo" ["Once a Moth"]. Adapted from a 1976 film with the same title, the play is set near a US military base in Pampanga province. Corazon de la Cruz wants to immigrate to America to work as a nurse. After her brother is shot— allegedly by accident—by an American soldier, she stays to seek justice, only to discover that the soldier has been reassigned to another country.

History would also be revisited in new works. Floy Quintos' "and St. Louis loves dem Filipinos," a play about the Igorot who were exhibited at the 1904 World's Fair, was staged in the 1990s by Dulaang Unibersidad ng Pilipinas [University of the Philippines Theater].

There were also new sarsuwela such as Nicanor Tiongson's 1982 "Pilipinas Circa 1907," about a pair of star-crossed lovers set against the backdrop of elections between pro- and anti-US political parties in the early years of American colonization; and Bienvenido Lumbera's 2001 "Hibik at Himagsik nina Victoria Lactao" ["Victoria Lactao and the Women's Cry and Revolt"], about Filipino women raped by American soldiers during the Philippine-American War.

Commenting on colonizations

Director Ricardo "Ricky" Abad's 2002 staging of "Ang Pagpapaamo sa Maldita," a Tagalog translation of Shakespeare's "The Taming of the Shrew" for Tanghalang Ateneo, a student theater group of Ateneo de Manila University, reconfigured the play's Italian characters into Filipinos and Americans.

The production is a commentary on and an amalgam of both Spanish and American colonial influences on Filipino theater: Shakespeare in English was taught to Filipinos by the Americans, the production used English and Tagalog for spoken lines, and the staging combined adapted forms of theater from both former colonizers.

Abad changed the setting of the play to a Philippine gold-mining town during the American occupation. Katharina was made into a Filipino native from a local wealthy family, while Petruchio was turned into an American soldier of fortune. "The play is now set to explore the dynamics of a colonial relationship, that of the American military officer and his taming of a native subject, Katharina the shrew," noted Abad.

Staging conventions from the (Spanish-influenced) sarsuwela were used together with (American-influenced) bodabil, reflecting how the latter eventually took over the former as the popular form of entertainment. "But it is the use of the traditions of seditious theater that this production finds its strongest anchor," he explained.

"Katharina and Petruchio are allegorical representations of the Philippines and America, and the taming process ... is the analogy for the kind of governance that the Americans imposed on the Filipinos at the time—a kind of paternal benevolence .... To the Americans, Filipinos were like children, full of great potential, but ones which were in great need of discipline. Like Katharina, we, Filipinos, are shrews that also must be tamed."[27]

Babes on Broadway

In 1943, composer Richard Rodgers and lyricist-dramatist Oscar Hammerstein II debuted their musical "Oklahoma!" to acclaim. This helped popularize book musicals (productions where book, lyrics, and choreography all work toward advancing characterizations and plot) and

[27] Abad, Ricardo. "Appropriating Shakespeare And Resisting Colonialism: Reflections of A Stage Director." Nagai, Hiroko and Valiente, Tito, eds. *Transnationalizing Culture in Asia: Dramas, Musics and Tourism Symposium*. Manila: Japan Foundation and Japanese Studies Program, Ateneo de Manila University. 2009.

usher in a popular era for Broadway that would last into the 1950s.

The pair went on to create three musicals that include Asian or Pacific Islander characters: Polynesian and Tonkinese/Vietnamese in "South Pacific" (1949), Siamese/Thai in "The King and I" (1951), and Chinese American in "Flower Drum Song" (1958).

These productions allowed US-born Barbara Luna and several Filipino American immigrants to debut on the Great White Way.

Barbara Luna (1939–) (also spelled BarBara) was born in New York to a Spanish Filipino father and an Italian Hungarian mother. When she was nine years old, Luna was cast as Ngana in "South Pacific," one of the two bi-racial children of a French plantation owner.

Set on a South Pacific island during WWII, the musical is about a white American nurse who falls in love with the plantation owner and struggles with her racial prejudice upon discovering he has children from his late Polynesian wife. (The Tonkinese character Bloody Mary was played by African American actor Juanita Hall; Bloody Mary's daughter Liat was played by white actor Betta St. John.)

Luna went on to play one of the royal children in "The King and I," a musical set in the 1860s about British teacher Anna Leonowens' experiences as a hired tutor for the King of Siam's children. (The King of Siam was played by Russian-born actor Yul Brynner.)

She was then cast as the understudy of Lotus Blossom, a role spoken completely in Japanese, in John Patrick's "Teahouse of the August Moon," a comedy about an American solider attempting to "Americanize" a Japanese town after WWII. She was eventually assigned the role for the show's national tour. Her other credits on Broadway include Anita in "West Side Story" and Diana Morales in "A Chorus Line."

Neile Adams (1932–), who was born in Manila and whose real name is Ruby Salvador Arrastia, moved to the US after WWII. Her mother Carmen "Miami" Salvador was a bodabil dancer in Manila. In 1953, Adams was cast in a feature dance role in "Kismet"—as one of The Three Princesses of Ababu—a musical about a wily poet who talks his way out of trouble.

In 1954, she took over the role of Gladys, a quick-witted secretary, in "The Pajama Game," a musical about a romance blossoming from opposite camps of a labor dispute at a pajama factory.

Manila-born Patrick Adiarte (1943–) was also cast as one of the royal children in "The King and I" until he graduated to playing the feature role of crown prince Chulalongkorn, eventually playing the same character in the 1956 film version.

He was later cast in "Flower Drum Song," a musical about Wang Ta, who struggles between following the customs of his Chinese roots and assimilating into American culture. Adiarte was cast as Wang San, Wang Ta's younger brother. He later reprised the role in the 1961 film version of the musical.

Cely Carrillo (1934–) (sometimes spelled Carillo in film and television credits) was a member of the UP Dramatic Club before moving to New York to study music at The Juilliard School under a scholarship. She began as an understudy for Mei Li, the love interest of Wang Ta, in "Flower Drum Song," and took over the role in 1960.

Maureen Tiongco (1935–) was born in Laguna province and was considered a triple threat—equally adept in acting, singing, and dancing—while still studying at UP.[28] She moved to New York after graduation to continue her dance training. She was in the dance ensemble of "Flower Drum Song" when it opened and eventually played Mei Li in the tour, taking over for Carrillo.

All five actors went on to work in American film and television.

---

[28] Cervantes, Behn. "How Maureen Tiongco conquered the US stage." *PDI*. Jan. 1, 2011.

2
Epiphanies
(1960s-1970s)

Identity and awakenings

From the 1960s to the 1970s, rock-'n'-roll music gave way to funk, which then gave way to disco and the beginnings of hip hop and rap. Television allowed news and entertainment programs to be widely distributed and accessed.

Broadway saw the arrival of the concept musicals (productions that do not necessarily have a plot), such as "Cabaret," "Hair," "Company," and "A Chorus Line." The Tony Awards began to be broadcast on television in 1967, helping create more awareness for theater, even though actual attendance to Broadway shows was declining due to worsening city conditions in New York. The award, founded by the American Theatre Wing 20 years earlier and given out for excellence in Broadway productions, is named after actor, director, and producer Antoinette Perry.

Off-Broadway theaters had emerged in the 1950s. Apart from the flexible aspects of geographical location, theater size and number of seats, and the more rigid parameters of salary range agreements with Actors' Equity Association (Equity), Off-Broadway shows are usually smaller in scale and budget, considered less commercial and more serious compared to the income-driven spectacles of Broadway fare.

Off-Off-Broadway productions, which took off in the 1960s, are considered non-profit ventures with a more experimental approach to material and staging. The Village Voice newspaper launched its Obie Awards in 1956 for Off-Broadway productions, with Off-Off-Broadway productions becoming eligible in 1964.

New York City was no longer considered the locus of professional theater in the US as regional theater companies started gaining traction across the country. In 1961, the Ford Foundation (established in 1936 by automobile manufacturer Henry Ford) provided funding to help new groups establish beginnings or to help existing groups grow. That same year, the foundation also formed the Theatre Communications Group to serve as an umbrella support organization for professional, community, and university theater groups.

In 1965, the National Endowment for the Arts was established to serve as an independent federal agency that provides funding for the arts. In 1966, the League of

Resident Theatres was formed to allow regional theaters to negotiate collectively with Equity.

The post-war conservative and compliant ways of the 1950s gave way to an anti-establishment counterculture. Alongside the anti-war movement against US involvement in the Vietnam War, social unrest among minority ethnic and identity groups focused the spotlight on pervasive inequality. Social movements and radical activism for civil rights and self-determination were prominent for African Americans, Asian Americans, Mexican Americans (Chicano Movement), Native Americans (American Indian Movement), women (Women's Liberation), and the gay community (Gay Liberation).

Filipino American and Asian American theater groups
A related result of the 1964 Civil Rights Act (which ended segregation in public places and prohibits discrimination based on race, color, religion, sex, or national origin) was the 1965 Immigration and Nationality Act, which removed much of the restrictions from previous immigration legislation. This allowed a new wave of Asians to immigrate to the US, including Filipinos.

In 1967, the student group Philippine (later Pilipino) American Collegiate Endeavor was established at San Francisco State College (later University). It went on to join other ethnic student groups to form the Third World Liberation Front. The coalition led student strikes from 1968 to 1969 at SF State and at University of California (UC)-Berkeley to demand for inclusion of ethnic-related subjects in school curricula. The strikes led to the establishment of the country's first Ethnic Studies department at UC Berkeley and the first College of Ethnic Studies at SF State.

One of the student groups that joined the coalition was the Asian American Political Alliance, founded in 1968 by Japanese American Yuji Ichioka and Chinese American Emma Gee. One of its goals was to unite different Asian ethnic groups by asserting their collective identity. The label "Asian American" was coined partly as a way to reject pejorative descriptions such as "Oriental."

Chinese and non-English language European ethnic theater groups had already been present in the US as early as the 1800s, though not always sustained. After a short rise in activity in the 1920s and 1930s, African American and Mexican American theater emerged again in the 1960s with groups such as Negro Ensemble Company in New York and El Teatro Campesino in Delano, California.

Amidst the backdrop of rising assertion of Asian American identity, four pioneering Asian American theater companies were founded in the US mainland: East West Players in Los Angeles, Northwest Asian American Theatre in Seattle, Asian American Theater Company in San Francisco, and Pan Asian Repertory Theatre in New York.

Lack of opportunities to play roles other than usually inconsequential or negative Asian stereotypes led Asian American theater artists to take matters into their own hands. These companies were not focused on Asian theater forms per se, rather, their ethos was American theater with and by Asian American theater makers. Filipino American theater artists were involved in all four companies, if not as founding members, then as pioneering or early collaborators.

Seminal Filipino American theater groups were formed in the late 1960s and the 1970s on opposite coasts of the US mainland as offshoots of social and political activism; and in Hawaii as an outgrowth from the education realm. The Filipino American theater makers involved with these groups used their knowledge of American and Filipino theater forms, dances, music, and languages to produce works that blended their experiences and cultures.

Studying and establishing

Several influential directors in Manila from the 1960s onward had opportunities to take higher studies in the US before establishing their careers.

Rolando Tinio (1937–97) studied creative writing at State University of Iowa. He was tasked to run the Ateneo Experimental Theater in 1960 at Ateneo de Manila University and direct its productions. He later founded Teatro Pilipino in '75 and went on to renew an interest in the local theater scene of translating plays in English to Filipino. His translations of American playwrights include Arthur Miller ("Death of a Salesman") and Tennessee Williams ("The Glass Menagerie").

Benjamin "Behn" Cervantes (1938–2013) took graduate studies in theater arts at University of Hawaii (UH) and drama and film at Columbia University and at Beloit College, Wisconsin. He became a founding member of Philippine Educational Theater Association in '67, and he founded University of the Philippines (UP) Repertory Company in '72. UP Repertory Company staged anti-government protest productions in Tagalog, such as "Estados Unidos versus Juan Matapang Cruz" ["United States versus Juan Matapang Cruz"], among others, for which Cervantes was frequently detained or imprisoned.

Antonio "Tony" Mabesa (1935–) finished his master's in theater arts at UC Los Angeles in '65, a master's in education at University of Delaware in '69, and was a teaching fellow while studying Asian and Western theater at UH Manoa from '70 to '73. He went on to teach at UP, founded school theater group Dulaang Unibersidad ng Pilipinas [University of the Philippines Theater] in '76, and later developed the school's undergraduate and graduate theater degree programs.

Two of the longest-surviving professional theater companies in Manila were founded by women who had studied in the US. Artists and workers from both groups have gone on to become involved in productions and theater groups in the US.

Zenaida Amador (1933–2004) studied drama at New York Academy of Dramatic Arts and taught drama and literature at University of South Dakota. She later received a grant from the US State Department's International Visitors Program to observe theater practices in Washington, DC and New York. She cofounded Repertory Philippines in '67, of which she was founding artistic director until her death. While its inaugural production was a Tagalog translation of August Strindberg's "Miss Julie," it has since staged English plays and musicals from America and Europe. Repertory

Philippines is known for having trained and developed countless actors in English-language theater, one of the most well-known being Lea Salonga.

Cecile Guidote-Alvarez (1943–) considered James Reuter, who had been one of her teachers at Saint Paul College in Manila, as a second father. He had given her a scholarship to the Ateneo Graduate Summer Drama Program, where she trained in theater work, and had endorsed her for scholarships for graduate studies in the US. She took up advanced theater studies at State University of New York-Albany on a Fulbright scholarship, and trained with actor-director Paul Baker at the Dallas Theater Center under a Rockefeller fellowship grant. During her studies in the US, she honed her thesis on "A Prospectus for the National Theater of the Philippines." Upon her return to Manila, Reuter offered her space in Ateneo's campus for the theater company that she founded in '67, Philippine Educational Theater Association (PETA).

PETA has gone on to become arguably the most well-known Filipino professional theater company that stages works in Tagalog. The group is also known for its advocacy of teaching theater making to different communities. Several of its alumni, carrying with them the pedagogical ethos of PETA, would go on to become involved in Filipino American theater.

East West Players in Los Angeles
East West Players (EWP) was founded in 1965 in Los Angeles by Makoto "Mako" Iwamatsu (founding artistic director), Rae Creevey, James Hong, June Kim, Guy Lee, Pat

Li, Yet Lock, Soon-Tek Oh, and Beulah Quo.

Pioneer member Alberto Isaac (1943–) was born in Leyte province, moved to the US in '61, and studied for a master's in drama at California State University-Los Angeles. He met Oh at an audition in '67, who invited him to join EWP. "I was cast as Soon-Tek's younger brother in a play ("Martyrs Can't Go Home") that he had written about the Korean War," said Isaac. "Through the years and in the three venues EWP occupied, I functioned in several capacities: as an actor, director, writer, literary manager, and, for a while, the theater's janitor."

"We performed in the basement of a church where Beulah Quo was a member," he said. "Several years later, we vacated the church after I did a nude scene in another play Soon-Tek had written ("Tondemonai—Never Happen!"). Beulah later said that shedding my clothes was a blessing in disguise because it forced the company to find its own physical theater space."

To counter the lack of material that includes Asian or Asian American characters, EWP launched an annual playwriting competition. In 1971, Chinese American Frank Chin's "The Chickencoop Chinaman" received first place. EWP was transferring locations at the time, so the play ended up being premiered at American Place Theatre in 1972 and is considered the first play written by an Asian American to have a major staging in New York City.

EWP also included Filipino American playwrights in its roster of productions. Two of Isaac's plays were part of its early seasons, followed by the plays of Dom Magwili and

Paul Stephen Lim through the mid-'70s to the '80s. Isaac's "How Juan Found His Fortune," based on a Filipino folktale where Juan outwits a menagerie of animals and a giant, was staged together with Glenn Johnson's "Urashima Taro," based on a Japanese folktale, in a twin bill titled "Tales of Juan and Taro" ('72). The production proved popular with young audiences and had stagings for several years.

Isaac also wrote "Coda," about a Filipino American woman and her gay Japanese American friend, both of whom fall in love with the same white American man. It was staged in a twin bill ('72) with Edward Sakamoto's "Yellow is My Favorite Color." Isaac recalled, "We had a good critical and box office response to the production. 'Coda' was later produced in San Francisco by the Asian American Theater Company and was also a critical and audience success."

"I am proud of having become a part of this pioneering company so early in its history," he said. "I like to think I contributed to its artistic growth and influence. I know it helped me develop as a person and, at the risk of sounding pretentious, as an artist. It opened my eyes to Asian American history and what still remains, despite some progress, the continuing artistic and political struggle of Asians in this country." Isaac continues to act and direct.

Ating Tao in San Francisco

In 1968, several students at SF State who were taking Ethnic Studies classes and/or were affiliated with Pilipino American Collegiate Endeavor (PACE) founded theater group Ating Tao [Our People]. The group collaboratively created shows that were comprised of skits focusing on

Filipino American identity, coupled with folk and modern dances, rhythm and blues and jazz music, and spoken poetry.

"We started off as a loose collective of different kinds of artists from poets to dancers," said Emilya Cachapero, who was a published poet and writer at the time. She performed poetry readings and would later shift to dance. "There were a variety of events during those times that combined poetry readings, music, and theater pieces. Ating Tao emerged from those events. What we were doing was a result and combination of culture politics and social action."

Luis "Lou" Syquia (1949–) said, "One of our skits was titled 'Coconut' because it referred to the idea that Filipino Americans are brown outside but white inside, that they are trying to follow another culture because they don't know who they are. We wanted to put together a production to show audiences that we could be proud of who we are.

"During those times, there were many ethnic groups going through the same process of asserting their identity and their contributions to society. There was no way for Filipino American students to find out about our identity and history other than through school because there were no books that talked about Filipinos in the US and their contributions. We liked to think that our show contributed to that in our small way."

Among other contributing writers who wrote skits for the group's productions were Syquia and his sibling Serafin and Oscar Peñaranda, all three of whom later went on to become published poets. Rosalie Alfonso served as choreographer and Benny Luis was one of the musicians. Directed by Don Marcos, the group's shows were staged in different colleges and universities in San Francisco and the Bay Area. The group toured as far south as San Diego and as far north as Seattle and was active until '72.

Dulaan ng mga Tao in Seattle

Born in Longbeach, California, Stan Asis (1945–) was studying drama at University of Washington (UW) in Seattle when he founded Dulaan ng mga Tao [Theater of the People] in 1971. "It was begun the same time I was theater manager at the university's Ethnic Cultural Center Theater (ECCT)," he said.

"The ECCT was a hotbed of drama and activism. It had visiting national figures sponsored by student groups. It featured community groups, individuals, speakers, and films. Many activities were steered by the Asian Student Coalition, Black Student Union, the Chicano students' MECHA (Movimiento Estudiantil Chicano de Aztlan [Chicano Student Movement of Aztlan]), and American Indian Student Movement."

"We did guerrilla theater," Asis said. The group performed original vignettes for the community at street fairs, colleges, and conferences. Some of their performances included "The Pinoy Lot," a satire about Filipino stereotypes adapted by Asis from Luis Valdez's "Los Vendidos" [Spanish for "The Sold Ones"]; and "Ameria" by Nemesio Domingo, Jr., a satire about the negative effects of western culture on Filipinos.

The group also held exhibitions of fight choreography and

even staged a puppet theater piece protesting the construction of the Kingdome Stadium and its impact on the elderly Filipino community in Seattle's International District. "These pieces came about because Pinoy students needed to express their needs and views," he said. The group was active for three years.

Endeavors in Hawaii

Born in Ilagan, Isabela province, Prescila "Precy" Espiritu (1937–) moved to Hawaii in 1967 and started teaching at UH Manoa in '71. She established the Ilocano Language Program for UH in '72 and it has since held annual festivals where students write and perform their own plays (drama or comedy), musicals, and sarsuwela in Ilocano.

"Students, in small groups, compete for cash prizes and trophies," she said. "The community is invited and a feast is enjoyed by everybody at the end of the event."

Pacita Saludes (1930–) founded Gunglo Dagiti Mannurat nga Ilokano iti Hawaii [Ilocano for "Association of Ilocano Writers in Hawaii"] (GUMIL Hawaii) in 1971 in Honolulu. The group stages productions written in Ilocano once a year. Born in Badoc, Ilocos Norte province, Saludes has written many plays that have been staged by the group.

The group's inaugural production in '75 was her "Gapu Ta Patpatgenka" ["Because You Are Dear To Me"], about a man who leaves his wife behind in the Philippines when he immigrates to Hawaii with his son. Though he falls in love with another woman, upon the prodding of his son, he finally petitions for his wife to join him.

Some of Saludes' other plays include "Uray Lakay No Landing" ["Even If He's Old When He Comes From Abroad"] ('89), about a retired man who returns to Ilocos to search for a bride; and "Bullalayaw Ti Ayat" ["Love Is A Rainbow"] ('92), about a couple who reunites after being apart for 17 years, among others.

GUMIL Hawaii has also staged the works of Mario Albalos (1950–91). Albalos, originally from Vigan, Ilocos Sur province, had joined the US Navy and then retired in Hawaii. Some of his plays include "Nailet ti Lubong" ["The World is Small"] ('79), "Adda Lunod Dagti Pasamak" ["Tragic Events"] ('81), and "Nasutil ti Lubong" ["The World is Unpredictable"] ('82), among others.

Tomas Hernandez (1946–) studied for a master's in dramatic art at UC Santa Barbara from '67 to '68 and for a doctorate in drama and theatre at UH Manoa from '71 to '75. While at Manoa, Hernandez translated Precioso Palma's sarsuwela "Paglipas ng Dilim" ["After the Darkness Passes"] into English as "Estrella." The production was directed by Tony Mabesa with music direction by Ricardo "Ric" Trimillos. Trimillos also conducted a rondalla to perform Leon Ignacio's music. "Estrella" had a run at the school campus and later toured the Big Island, Maui, and Kauai.

The individuals involved in the production decided to set up Tanghalan Repertory Theatre [Performance Repertory Theatre] with Hernandez as their director. The group went on to stage other sarsuwela and poetry readings. It also staged plays written by Filipinos in English such as the works of playwright Nick Joaquin and an adaptation of writer and poet Jose Garcia Villa's short story "Mir I Nisa," about the titular Muslim princess and her two suitors.

The group disbanded in 1980 when Hernandez relocated. After several years teaching in the academe, he went on to work as Performing Arts Director for the Arizona Commission on the Arts, then as director of the Opera-Musical Theater Program at the National Endowment for the Arts, before becoming a concert producer for the Library of Congress.

Grand Guignol in the Philippines

In 1972, during what should have been his second and last term as president, Ferdinand Marcos imposed martial law in the Philippines. Civil rights were suspended and tens of thousands of critics, activists, dissidents, and other perceived enemies of the state were arrested without warrants, detained, tortured, incarcerated, disappeared, or extrajudicially executed. Victims included students, academics, labor group organizers, white collar professionals, journalists, and theater artists, among others. Widespread cronyism across industries and embezzlement of public funds plunged the country into record levels of poverty and debt. This corrupt and violent dictatorship would go on to last for more than a decade.[29]

Some martial law emigrants to the US would later on become involved in Filipino American theater, such as playwright and director Ralph Peña, who went on to cofound Ma-Yi Theater in New York in 1989, and director Jon Lawrence Rivera, who went on to cofound Playwrights'

---

[29] Francia, Luis. *A History of the Philippines: From Indios Bravos to Filipinos*. New York: Overlook Press. 2010.

Arena in Los Angeles in 1992. After Rivera's journalist father was blacklisted by the dictatorship in the '70s, their family took asylum in Australia before Rivera made his way to the US. Peña left for the US after he'd been called in for questioning by the military for his work with a protest theater group. The parents of Jose Llana, Melody Butiu, and Jaygee Macapugay all left the Philippines because of martial law. All three actors would go on to perform in "Here Lies Love," a musical about first lady Imelda Marcos, in the 2010s.

Philippine Educational Theatre Arts League in New York

After martial law was imposed, Cecile Guidote was on the regime's radar because not only did she turn down Imelda Marcos' invitation to be the artistic director of the Cultural Center of the Philippines, she had also publicly questioned the conjugal dictators' use of a war damage fund that had been authorized by the US Congress (Philippine Rehabilitation Act of 1946) toward the center's construction. Also, her boyfriend at the time, politician Heherson "Sonny" Alvarez, was wanted by the regime under a shoot-to-kill order.

Soldiers started to show up where she worked. "I was worried for the safety of the artists. I did not want the PETA productions to be stopped. We wanted to proceed as normally as possible," she wrote in a piece for Philippine Daily Inquirer.

At one point, she received a phone call from Ellen Stewart, African American founder of La MaMa Experimental

Theatre Club in New York City. The pair had met when Stewart visited Manila previously in '71 as a UNESCO (United Nations Educational, Scientific and Cultural Organization) ambassador to the Philippines.

Stewart asked why Guidote had not responded to an invitation to become a consultant for the International Theatre Institute (the global theater network organization established by UNESCO in 1948). That was when Guidote realized her mail was being intercepted.

She and Alvarez married in secret that year, officiated by James Reuter, prior to Alvarez's escape to the US. For her spouse's fake passports, she used the names of two of her actors from PETA. She flew to the US in 1973.

In New York, she reconnected with Stewart and established the Philippine Educational Theatre Arts League (Petal) at La MaMa. For the group, she conceived and directed dance-based productions, often working with dancers and choreographers Reynaldo "Ronnie" Alejandro and Ricci Reyes (later Reyes-Adan).

She also directed or acted in plays such as "Kuwintas ni Lumnay" ["Lumnay's Necklace"], adapted from Amador Daguio's story "Wedding Dance," about a woman left by her husband because they are unable to conceive; "Sundalo" ["Soldier"], adapted from Sister Angela Barrios' play "Hello Soldier," where Gina and her mother pin their hopes of escaping poverty on the American WWII soldier who fathered Gina; and "Pet for Company," Alex Swanbeck's play about a couple's argument, adapted by Guidote-Alvarez to a Filipino American setting; among others.

She also served as director of the Third World Institute of Theatre Arts Studies, which was hosted by La MaMa. "We linked up to undertake cultural events for the United Nations conferences," she wrote. The institute was designed to foster cross-cultural exchange between Third World and minority artists from the United States and featured artists and works from India, Indonesia, Japan, Suriname, and Uganda, among others. Guidote-Alvarez and her family eventually returned to the Philippines in '86 after the Marcos family was deposed.[30]

Sining Bayan in Berkeley

In 1974, Sining Bayan [People's Art] was formed as the cultural arm of activist group Katipunan ng mga Demokratikong Pilipino (KDP) [Union of Democratic Filipinos]. The group recruited volunteer actors and crew from the community and staged skits, one-act plays, and full theatrical productions.

Born in Berkeley, California, Ermena Marlene Vinluan (1949–) had been studying at UC Berkeley for a year when she left to study in Manila. During her year and a half there, she began to become exposed to pressing sociopolitical issues of the times. She returned to a more politicized and more diverse Berkeley campus. By then, it had already opened its ethnic studies department and its drama department had started staging productions with anti-war and anti-racist themes. In 1973, John Silva and Bruce Occena, instructors of her Philippine Studies class,

---

[30] Guidote-Alvarez, Cecile. "Love and marriage in the time of martial law (Part 1)." *PDI*. Sept. 24, 2015.; "Love in the time of martial law: The escape (Part 2)." *PDI*. Sept. 25, 2015.

recruited her to co-write and direct a historical pageant, "Isuda ti Immuna" [Ilocano for "Those Who Were First"]. Loosely based on Carlos Bulosan's "America is in the Heart," the pageant combined songs, skits, and poetry.

"I'd liked theater since writing and directing my own little productions in elementary school and throughout high school," she said. Vinluan had also taken workshops with El Teatro Campesino and Peter Brooke's International Centre for Theatre Research. She had also trained at the American Academy of Dramatic Art in Pasadena, California.

In joining KDP, Vinluan combined her passion for theater with activism and she became Sining Bayan's artistic director. "Sining Bayan aimed to educate and organize its audiences," she said. "Its members were mostly college students and young workers. We also had high school students, Vietnam War vets, and grandparents. It was a wide range of different kinds of people. In some productions, Sining Bayan also included several professional actors, musicians, and dancers, but mostly, our members were inexperienced, amateur performers whose hard work, dedication, natural talents, and rigorous rehearsals often yielded polished performances and invariably gave audiences inspired, spirited stage shows."

Sining Bayan went on to restage "Isuda" several times. It staged "Maguindanao" ('74), later retitled "Mindanao," which focused on Muslim Filipinos; and "Sakada" ('75), about plantation workers in the Philippines. Most of the group's other productions tackled Filipino American issues: the elderly in "Tagatupad" ["Those Who Must Carry On"] ('76); war brides who immigrated to the US after WWII in

"War Brides" ('79); and immigrant plantation workers in Hawaii in "Ti Mangyuna" [Ilocano for "Those Who Led the Way"], its last production, in 1981. After the group disbanded, Vinluan went on to work in film.

The group toured its shows in cities where KDP had chapters such as Seattle, San Francisco, Los Angeles, Chicago, Washington, DC, Philadelphia, New York, and Honolulu, among others. "Sining Bayan performed in a range of venue types. From community centers to high school auditoriums, grade school cafetoriums, high-end university and professional theaters, and even an Irish pub in San Francisco at the invitation of local members of the IRA (Irish Republican Army)," Vinluan said.

"Our audiences were mostly Filipino Americans because that was our base, as well as our outreach. But KDP also had extensive non-Filipino networks throughout the various political organizations and communities, so our audiences included activists or members from peace organizations, leftist movements, church groups, student networks, Latinos, Asians, Blacks, Mid-Eastern communities, and others."

In 1977, Sining Bayan staged "The Frame-up of Narciso and Perez," about immigrant nurses Filipina Narciso and Leonora Perez, to raise awareness for the circumstantial case accusing the pair of murdering patients at a Veterans Administration hospital in Ann Arbor, Michigan. The production was part of KDP's campaign against the trial, which included protests in several major cities. The nurses were later pronounced innocent and released.

Leonora's son Jason Magabo Perez has written semi-autobiographical one-person multimedia plays "The Passion of El Hulk Hogancito" (2009), where third-grade student Hason muses on his wrestling heroes while attempting to understand his mother, a Filipina nurse who has been framed for murder; and "You Will Gonna Go Crazy" (staged as a work-in-progress in 2011), where an adult Hason confronts "intimacy, violence, patriarchy, and the traumatic impacts of racism and sexism on the Filipino American family." Both works were premiered by dance and music ensemble Kulintang Arts in San Francisco.[31]

Northwest Asian American Theatre in Seattle

In 1972, Timoteo "Tim" Cordova and Nemesio Domingo, Jr., with Chinese American Douglas Chin, founded the Asian Multi Media Center (AMMC) in Seattle as an acting group. By the following year, the group expanded its thrust to provide training for inner city youth in acting, photography, graphic arts, etc. The objective was to help expose participants to the possibilities of working in the mass communications professions.

AMMC was initially formed as a subgroup under Filipino Youth Activities, an organization founded by Cordova's parents Dorothy and Fred in '57 to provide "wholesome activities that would also teach Filipino culture" to children, which included sports, parade drill marching, and folk dancing. Among other civic engagements, Dorothy and Fred (who had been adopted as a child by Lucia "Lucing"

---

[31] Perez, Jason. "Prefatory notes re: U.S. v. Narciso and Perez (1977)." Jason Perez website: Jasonmagaboperez.com. Undated.
http://jasonmagaboperez.com/us-vs-narciso-perez

Cordova) went on to found the Filipino American National Historical Society in 1982.

In 1974, AMMC held an acting workshop taught by drama students from University of Washington (UW), which included Stan Asis and Japanese American Marilyn Tokuda, both of whom were actively exploring the dynamics of Asian American theater. Asis noted that the university's Ethnic Cultural Center Theater was a "cauldron of ethnic cultural events" and that it helped ignite "the fervor to develop and search for relevant materials."

Asis had previously produced a trilogy of Philippine plays. He had also conceived and directed the mime production "Makisig," adapted from Gemma Cruz (later Araneta)'s children's book "Makisig: The little hero of Mactan."

For UW's Filipino Student Association, he had directed Amelia Lapeña-Bonifacio's "The Short, Short Life of Citizen Juan." The play, which was produced by Maria Batayola, is about a man whose life is complicated when he runs for public office upon the prodding of his townmates.

"During those times, Marilyn, Maria and I expressed our need for an Asian theater group," he said. That same year, with support from AMMC, the three of them and UW drama students Yolly Irigon, Gloria Pacis, Henry Tonel, and Chinese American Larry Wong established Theatrical Ensemble of Asians (TEA).

That November, Asis wrote and directed TEA's inaugural production "Philippine Legends, Folklore and American Impressions," based on Carlos Bulosan's works.

Asis served as TEA's unofficial first artistic director until he relocated to San Francisco and Irigon became the interim artistic director. The group moved out of the university in '75, formally joined AMMC, changed its name to Asian Exclusion Act, and hired Japanese American Garrett Hongo as the artistic director. After AMMC closed in '77, the theater group struck out on its own, then changing its name again to Northwest Asian American Theatre in '81.

The group stayed active until 2004. Productions featuring the works of Filipino American playwrights include Mel Escueta's "Honey Bucket" (1976–77 season), Batayola's adaptation of "Gathering Ground" ('85–'86), Batayola and Chris Wong's "Love Sutras" ('89–'90), Asis' "Monkey King: The Transformation" ('90–'91), and Ralph Peña's "Flipzoids" ('99–'00), among others.

Asian American Theater Company in San Francisco

With support from the American Conservatory Theater (ACT), Frank Chin founded the Asian American Theater Workshop in San Francisco in 1973 to train Asian Americans in acting and playwriting. In '75, the workshop became an independent entity and was renamed the Asian American Theater Company (AATC).

Melvyn "Mel" Escueta's (1945–99) "Honey Bucket" was one of the first Filipino American-written plays staged by the group. AATC produced it in '75 and again in '79. Escueta was born in Manila, enlisted in the Marines in '65, and was deployed to Vietnam the year after. He later "channeled the anguish of his experiences" from the Vietnam War into his play about Filipino American Andy Bonifacio—who is guilt-ridden after having killed his fellow Asians in Vietnam.[32]

Other plays written by Filipino Americans produced by the group include Dom Magwili's "Manila Murders" ('77) and Oscar Peñaranda's one-acts "The Truant," a tragicomedy about a young man who wants to drop out of college, and "Followers of the Seasons," about workers in a fish cannery in Alaska (both in '79). Also in '79 was Alberto Isaac's "Coda," and Paul Stephen Lim's one-act "Points of Departure." The company continued to feature Filipino American playwrights throughout the decades until it was dissolved in 2011.

The company was eventually run by an artistic committee, with different members rotating as the committee chair. Emilya Cachapero was part of the committee from '76 until the mid-'80s. In addition to her administrative, acting, and directing work for AATC, she was also cofounder of the Pilipino Artists Center, an organization that provided arts workshops for youth in writing, dance, and music. Her work there eventually grew into her involvement with Diwa [Essence], a multi-genre Filipino American artist collective, and later, its offshoot dance group Bagong Diwa [New Essence].

Cachapero also founded the San Francisco Ethnic Dance Festival in 1978. "We wanted to recognize the diverse populations in the San Francisco area and celebrate those cultures," she said. Cachapero later went on to work as an administrator for the ACT. After moving to New York, she

[32] Fabros, Alex. "A Teacher, Mentor, Fellow Marine, and My Friend." Phil-Am Bahay Kubo website: Philipppines.tripod.com. Undated. http://philipppines.tripod.com/escueta.html

joined the Theatre Communications Group in '91 as the Director of Artistic Programs and International Theatre Institute-US.

Turned upside down

Domingo "Dom" Albert Magwili (1949–) was born in Alameda, California. After studying communication arts at University of San Francisco, he trained at ACT from '72 to '74 and then at EWP starting 1974.

During his time at ACT, he did not engage with the Asian American Theater Workshop. "At the time, I still thought of myself as more European than Asian American, much less being Pilipino. In those days, such terms were not in common use; and those notions were beyond me," he said. "After I'd completed my training at ACT, I wanted to move on to the next step. My plan was to do two years in Los Angeles then move to New York."

He went to watch a production by EWP only because he had mutual agents with Mako Iwamatsu. "I did so with a lot of resistance and bad attitude. I was firmly convinced that I was one of maybe five trained 'Oriental' actors in the US. What need had I to see a small community theater group when I had already performed on the great Geary Theater in San Francisco? Remember, in those days I thought I was white," he said.

He caught EWP's production of "In the Jungle of Cities." "My world turned upside down. There were some 30, it seemed to me, Asian American actors performing Brecht, without accents. It was a competent production. I suddenly realized that I was not the only one." He volunteered to be an usher, then moved on to become a stage manager, playwright, and understudy actor. "Eventually, I directed my first play, Ed Sakamoto's 'That's the Way the Fortune Cookie Crumbles' and I was on my way."

Though his long-term focus was on acting, Magwili delved into playwriting as well. "At the time, I was discontented. I was still processing my place as a new actor in EWP, and myself as an Asian American artist. I saw the shows at EWP to be very political but not particularly humane. It seemed the writers of the time were more interested in stating political doctrine and not exploring insights into the human condition. They took themselves very seriously and weren't any fun," he said. In 1976, he wrote the comedy "Nobody On My Side of the Family Looks Like That!" for EWP's playwriting competition. "I wrote it to laugh and poke fun at those writers," he explained.

EWP provided Magwili with opportunities to recalibrate his sense of identity. In one acting class, his spouse Saachiko suggested he use a Filipino accent. "It was the first time I actively used the Pilipino dialect in my acting. I was in my mid-20s. I had never used that dialect for fear of embarrassing myself. Mako and my classmates erupted in amazement and laughter.

"It was a breakthrough for me. EWP was my gateway into finding my Pilipino American self. I was so young then, in life experience, in skills, in expectations. I was very grateful for that experience. I started defining for myself what a Pilipino American is. [Since then,] I started actively writing Pilipino American material. And I still do to this day."

Magwili eventually became involved with AATC in '77. "Since my family lived in Oakland, it was an easy trek to their theater. I was writing and teaching acting for them during that time for pocket money." Frank Chin approached him to write a play, which resulted in Magwili's second play "Manila Murders," a pot boiler mystery that takes place in the Philippines during martial law. Magwili went on to write several more plays for EWP well into the mid-'80s. Based in Los Angeles, he continues to act, teach, and direct.

*

Paul Stephen Lim (1944–) had already dropped out of college and had been working as an advertising copywriter in Manila when he decided to relocate to the US in '69. He resumed his undergraduate studies at University of Kansas, where a theater professor inspired him to transform a short story he had written into a play.

The result, "Conpersonas," earned Best Original Script from the 1976 National Student Playwriting Awards and received a staging at the American College Theatre Festival organized by the John F. Kennedy Center for the Performing Arts in Washington, DC.

Lim went on to write more plays: "Points of Departure" ('78) and "Mother Tongue" ('88), produced at EWP; "Woeman" ('78) and "Flesh, Flash and Frank Harris" ('80) produced at Off-Broadway theaters. When "Conpersonas" received the student playwriting award, the prize included representation by the William Morris Agency in New York. Lim's agent advised him to capitalize on and write about his "unique Asian background."

Lim didn't want to be pigeonholed as an "ethnic writer" and refused. His "Mother Tongue," he concedes in an essay on his website, is his "one and only play which draws almost completely on my own unique Asian background." The play is about a university professor who uncovers truths about his relationships and himself as he writes a play about his mother—who had been a child-bride from China married off to an older man in the Philippines in the late 1930s. Ironically, it's also his most-produced play. He wrote, "Is it really a better play [compared to my other plays] or are audiences more willing to embrace [it] because it's an Asian American play by an Asian American playwright?"[33]

Pan Asian Repertory Theatre in New York

In 1977, Chinese American Tisa Chang established Pan Asian Repertory Theatre (PAR) in New York City. Ernest Hawkins Abuba (1947–), who was married to Chang at the time, was a founding member. Abuba, whose father is Filipino, was born in Honolulu. He studied at Actor's Stage Studio in Washington, DC before relocating to New York, where he became a member of Off-Off-Broadway group Theatre Unlimited.

Abuba was cast in the world premiere of Stephen Sondheim's "Pacific Overtures" ('76), a musical about the westernization of Japan and considered the first Broadway production to consciously cast Asian American actors in Asian roles. He also performed for other groups, including

[33] Lim, Paul Stephen. "Embracing or Erasing Race?" Paul Stephen Lim website: PaulStephenLim.com. Oct. 22, 2009. http://paulstephenlim.com/archives/731

Third World Institute of Theatre Arts Studies in its staging of "Caucasian Chalk Circle" ('77) at La MaMa.

He wrote several plays that graced PAR's early seasons, including "The Dowager" ('79) and "An American Story" ('80), where a Filipino immigrant confronts disillusionment in a bar in San Diego's Manilatown during Christmas in 1963 (partly inspired by the milieu of his own childhood upbringing in San Diego).

In '83, he received an Obie Award for Performance for his work as Captain Kenji Kadota in PAR's staging of Rick Shiomi's comedy mystery "Yellow Fever." In '84, his "American Story" was staged by AATC in San Francisco, directed by Emilya Cachapero. That same year, he wrote "Eat a Bowl of Tea" for PAR, his adaptation of Chinese immigrant Louis Chu's 1961 novel of the same title.

Abuba has gone on to act in or direct many of PAR's productions as well as with other groups such as National Asian American Theater Company. He has been a faculty member of Sarah Lawrence College since 1995.

*

Also in 1977, Cynthia Carrillo Onrubia, daughter of Cely Carrillo, was cast in the Broadway musical "A Chorus Line" at 15 years old. She would return to the show several times during its run, playing different characters.

Onrubia has gone on to act in, assist in choreographing, or choreographing other Broadway productions, including playing Victoria in the original cast of the musical "Cats" ('82) and Kitty in "Damn Yankees" ('94).

Philippine martial law onstage

The Marcos-imposed martial law years and dictatorship have been tackled on US stages. The highlighted figure, however, is usually Ferdinand's spouse Imelda, who has gained infamy for, among other things, her extravagance (multimillion-dollar shopping sprees in Manhattan, owning thousands of pairs of shoes, etc.).

Dogeaters

"Dogeaters" by Jessica Hagedorn, adapted from her 1990 novel of the same title, premiered in 1998 at La Jolla Playhouse, San Diego. Through the eyes of Rio Gonzaga, who has returned to Manila from the US, the play explores the Philippines in 1982 as a dictator regime unravels.

It was staged Off-Broadway in 2001 at The Public Theater (The Public) and then in Los Angeles by Playwrights' Arena in 2004 at Kirk Douglas Theater directed by Jon Lawrence Rivera.

It had its San Francisco premiere in 2016 by Magic Theatre. Included in that cast were Ogie Zulueta, who had worked on the play in the 1997 workshop, and Rinabeth Apostol, who would be performing the material for the first time.

"In the workshop, I was asked to read for the role of Joey Sands, a streetwise hustler with an American GI father and Filipino mother. And luckily, I was hired," said Zulueta, who was born in Manila and moved to San Francisco with his family when he was two years old.

For the 2016 production, he was cast to play other roles. "It makes sense for me to mature into the older characters. My approach to this project will be the same as I approach any other play. I treat it as a new play and try and rediscover the material with the talent in the room, that way my approach stays fresh and immediate," he said.

To prepare for her role as Rio, Apostol researched the martial law years by interviewing her parents, both of whom were activists in the Philippines in the 1980s. Born in San Francisco, Apostol also mined her own perspectives. "I use a lot of personal experiences from when I visited the Philippines. I find I can relate a lot to what the character of Rio observes," she said.

Both actors said they admire Hagedorn's novel. "I was blown away by the storytelling, language and power of the novel, especially that it's an acclaimed novel about the Philippines," said Zulueta. Apostol said, "I'm a huge fan. I was so eager to revisit the book, to provide insight and be reminded of details that aren't necessarily written into the play version."[34]

Imelda: A New Musical

East West Players staged "Imelda: A New Musical" in 2005 at its David Henry Hwang Theater, with a book by Sachi Oyama, music by Nathan Wang, and lyrics by Aaron Coleman. Spanning from the 1940s to the 1980s, the musical follows Imelda's ascent to power and eventual deposing.

It earned the largest one-week gross of ticket sales for EWP at the time.[35] In the cast were Liza Del Mundo as Imelda

---

[34] Ang. "Hagedorn's 'Dogeaters' to open in San Francisco in February." *Inquirer.net.* Jan. 19, 2016. http://globalnation.inquirer.net/135295/135295
[35] Nepales, Ruben. "East West Players toast artistic director." *PDI.* Aug. 2, 2013.

Marcos, Giovanni Ortega as Ferdinand Marcos, Antoine Diel as Marcos' political rival Benigno "Ninoy" Aquino, Jr., and Myra Cris Ocenar as Benigno's spouse Corazon "Cory" Aquino.

The musical was premiered in New York in 2009 by PAR at Julia Miles Theatre. The cast included Jaygee Macapugay as Imelda, Mel Sagrado Maghuyop as Ferdinand, Brian Jose as Ninoy, and Liz Casasola as Cory.

Here Lies Love

"Here Lies Love," a musical about the life of Imelda set in a disco where audiences stand and move around with the actors, opened Off-Broadway in 2013. It earned an Obie Award for music (David Byrne and Norman "Fatboy Slim" Cook) and lyrics (Byrne).

In a 2007 developmental concert version at Carnegie Hall, Joan Almedilla played Imelda. The original 2013 cast included Jose Llana as Ferdinand, Conrad Ricamora as Ninoy, and Melody Butiu as Imelda's nanny Estrella Cumpas. When the show moved to The Public for a 2014–15 run, Jaygee Macapugay took over the role of Imelda.

"The songs are a truncated anthology of Imelda's life up until the People Power Revolution," said Chicago-native Macapugay. "It seemed as if her life had its own soundtrack. David was fascinated by Imelda installing a disco ball in one of her New York City residences. He was fascinated with the idea of how extremely powerful people live in their own bubble."

Butiu had been involved with the musical since it was still

in its concept-album phase in 2005, while Macapugay had played Imelda previously in PAR's staging of "Imelda: A New Musical."

Llana, Macapugay, and Butiu's respective parents left the Philippines because of martial law. Both actresses researched to prepare for their roles, from reading books and news articles to interviewing people who had spent time with the Marcoses.

Macapugay considered filmmaker Ramona Diaz's 2003 documentary "Imelda" as a great resource. "Seeing and hearing Imelda discuss in her own words her personal account of her rise to power and her overall life philosophy was fascinating and extremely helpful in creating the character," she said.

Butiu reread Carmen Navarro-Pedrosa's "The Untold Story of Imelda Marcos." "It has the most detailed account of my character, Estrella Cumpas," she said.

Born in New York and raised in Washington state, Butiu said she hardly saw any Filipino stories on television and in the movies when she was growing up. "And certainly not in theater," she added. "To have the opportunity to tell Filipino stories on stage is a chance to delve into my family's history with my art. It's awesome to know that Filipinos in the audience can see their perspectives being shared, but also that others can see the universality in our experiences. Filipino stories are human stories."[36]

---

[36] Ang. "Filipino-Americans lead in Seattle staging of 'Here Lies Love'." *Inquirer.net.* Mar. 15, 2017. http://usa.inquirer.net/2169/fil-ams-lead-seattle-staging-lies-love

Pilipino Cultural Night

An increase in Filipino immigrants to America, and thus an increase in the number of Filipino students and teachers, and the opening of ethnic or Asian American studies programs in colleges and universities, are both contributing factors to the emergence in the 1970s of what has become an annual tradition: the Pilipino Cultural Night, popularly known as PCN.

Produced and performed by Filipino American student organizations, PCNs are annual cultural variety shows staged on campuses, predominantly in the West Coast where there are larger Filipino American populations. A show typically includes song numbers (sometimes including Filipino folk songs or classical ballads) and dance suites with skits in-between to thread the show's elements together.

The skits or play script have evolved to follow a common theme of focusing on and introducing Philippine and Filipino American history as a way to partly contextualize Filipino American identity.

The dance numbers are linked to the repertoire of Bayanihan Dance Company, a national dance company in the Philippines. ["Bayanihan" is Tagalog for the tradition of "communal solidarity" or "shared labor."]

Helena Benitez, who founded the company in the late 1950s, tasked Lucrecia Urtula to adapt regional and indigenous ritual and ceremonial dances from across the Philippines (usually outdoors, sometimes days-long) into choreographed pieces for the stage (indoors, with time limits). Lucrecia Kasilag was tasked to adapt and compose music to accompany the pieces.

After debuting internationally at the 1958 Brussels World's Fair, Bayanihan made several appearances in the US, including on the television program "The Ed Sullivan Show." Former members who have immigrated to the US have passed on the company's institutionalized choreography to many generations of amateur and professional dancers.

For some Filipino Americans, watching or being part of a PCN serves as their first exposure to Filipino American theater or performing arts. Actor and director Allan Manalo and playwright Conrad Panganiban, both affiliated with Bindlestiff Studio, were inspired to continue in the performing arts after joining their first PCNs. In 1997, Manalo's sketch-comedy troupe tongue in A mood staged a successful run of "PCN Salute," its parody of the PCN milieu.

3
Establish
(1980s–1990s)

Establishing more Filipino American theater groups
Synthesized music, rhythm and blues, punk and new wave, and heavy metal music in the 1980s would give way to grunge and electronic dance music in the '90s. Cassette tapes would give way to music CDs (compact discs), which in turn, would give way to digital music files. Ceaseless access to cable television would be joined by the newfound possibilities of the World Wide Web.

In the 1880s–1890s, operettas by British duo composer Arthur Sullivan and librettist William Schwenck Gilbert such as "The Pirates of Penzance" and "The Mikado" were popular in the US. Mirroring that trend, what dominated Broadway in the 1980s–1990s were imported British spectacle-driven, sung-through musicals—or what has become known as megamusicals—such as "Cats," "Les Miserables," and "The Phantom of the Opera." Later on, stage adaptations of live and animated films became the trend, with shows such as "Disney's Beauty and the Beast," "Disney's The Lion King," "Footloose," and "Saturday Night Fever." Shows with commercial, family-friendly mass appeal and efforts made by New York City's local government to clean up the area helped attract audiences back to Broadway.

During these two decades, Filipino American theater makers established or reconfigured quite a number of companies. Surviving groups that focus on or initially focused on Filipino American identity and works include Ma-Yi Theater in New York, CIRCA-Pintig (originally Pintig Cultural Group) in Chicago, and Bindlestiff Studio in San Francisco.

Awareness for Asian American theater artists received a boost when Chinese American playwright David Henry Hwang's "M. Butterfly" opened on Broadway in 1988. His play about the relationship between Song Liling, a male Chinese spy disguised as a female opera singer, and a male French diplomat, went on to receive the Tony Award for Best Play. The play gave Chinese American actor Bradley Darryl "BD" Wong the opportunity to receive a Tony Award—for Best Actor in a Play—for his work as Song.

Hwang has a Philippine connection. Though his mother was born in Xiamen, a city in China's Fujian province, she grew up in the Philippines. Born in Los Angeles, Hwang visited his maternal grandmother in Cebu, Philippines when he was 10 years old and recorded her memories of her father.

The notes would later be used as material for his play "Golden Child," where a Fujianese man returns to his family in China after years of doing business in the Philippines.

San Francisco-native Alec Mapa (1965–) was the Song understudy while playing another role in "M. Butterfly." He eventually replaced Wong—playing Song until 1990, and then in the national tour until 1991. As part of the tour's publicity to promote mystery around Song's actual gender, Mapa was billed as "A. Mapa."

In high school, Mapa was inspired by a teacher to focus on his talents for comedy and acting. Mapa went on to study drama at New York University before venturing into theater work. He has gone on to establish a career in stand-up comedy and works in film and television as well.

A boost for awareness of Filipino American theater artists came from the casting of Filipino actor Lea Salonga in the Broadway musical "Miss Saigon" in 1991.

Another boost came a few years later when Paolo Montalban (1973–) was cast as the Prince in the 1997 television adaptation of Rodgers and Hammerstein's musical "Cinderella." The show gained attention for its multiracial cast and because of the fame of one of its producers, celebrity singer Whitney Houston.

Montalban was born in Manila and moved to New York City with his family when he was a year old. He later reprised his role in a 2000–2001 US tour of the musical. Montalban continues to act in productions across the country.

Filipino American theater educators

Formal instruction of theater-related disciplines in the US academe began when George Pierce Baker started teaching a playwriting class at Harvard University in 1905. Thomas Woods Stevens founded the first college drama department in 1914 at Carnegie Institute of Technology (later Carnegie Mellon University). Baker went on to found Yale University's School of Drama in 1925.

Filipino Americans in theater education include Marilyn Abad-Cardinalli (1947–), who was born in San Jose, California and took up a master's in theater arts and related technology at San Jose State University. She started teaching theater at Gavilan College in Gilroy, California in '72. She directed and produced over a hundred productions during her 37 years there, where she was also a writer, designer, and television executive producer.

In '85, she founded Summer Theatre Arts Repertory (later renamed STAR Arts Education) to provide theater and video arts programs for young people. "My decision to be in educational theater was most rewarding and the best choice for me because I chose to be a teacher," she said. "I was able to create theater, inspire young men and women, and work with some of the most talented theater artists." She has also been a board member of El Teatro Campesino since 1991.

Edgardo de la Cruz (1933–2004), who was raised in Los Baños, Laguna province, studied for a master's in theater at University of Hawaii (UH)-Manoa, where he staged Nick Joaquin's "A Portrait of the Artist as Filipino" for his thesis. He started teaching at California State University-Hayward in '81, where he eventually became head of its directing program. Many of his students would go on to receive awards at the American College Theatre Festival's regional and national competitions. He authored the book "Directing for Theater: A Personal Approach" (2004).[37]

Ann Fajilan (1955–) was born in Albuquerque, New Mexico; completed her master's in directing at University of California (UC)-Davis in '82; then moved to San Francisco and worked for different theater companies, including Asian American Theater Company (AATC), in different capacities such as stage manager, production manager, and director.

"Some of the challenges of being an American Filipina," during that time, she said, "was that we were very scarce in the mainstream theater and were viewed as the 'utility' Asian. It was also a very male-dominated scene with a few Asian American females breaking the barriers with important works." The odds did not deter her. She taught at City College of San Francisco for 18 years where she was the artistic producing director of the Festival of American Playwrights of Color from 1996 to 2006.

Fajilan has also worked on adapting and directing oral histories and memoirs for the stage such as "Seven Card Stud with Seven Manangs Wild," based on the 2002 anthology of Filipino American writing; and "Twenty Five Chickens and a Pig," from Evangeline Buell's 2006 book "Twenty Five Chickens and a Pig for a Bride: Growing Up in a Filipino Immigrant Family."

---

[37] Rubentsein, Steve. "Edgardo de la Cruz- avid theater teacher, dedicated mentor." *San Francisco Chronicle*. July 14, 2004.

In 1989, playwright Paul Stephen Lim became a faculty member of University of Kansas. He established English Alternative Theatre the following year to develop and stage his students' new plays. It lasted for 21 years until his retirement. In 1996, Lim was awarded a gold medallion by the John F. Kennedy Center for the Performing Arts for his work with student playwrights.

In 1990, Ruth Mabanglo (1949–) moved to Hawaii from the Philippines to teach Tagalog language classes under UH's Filipino and Philippine Literature program, which was founded in 1963 by Teresita Ramos.

"Since drama is a wonderful technique in teaching foreign languages, Ramos used it as a culminating activity for her classes," said Mabanglo, who went on to reconfigure the recitals of the program's different classes into an annual drama festival held during the spring.

"We have a theme each year and students write original scripts, mostly collaborative, to test their writing proficiency based on the theme. Each play would not be more than 20 minutes. The program has multiple levels and classes. In the festival, classes from the same level compete with each other." In 1996, a song festival was launched, held annually during the fall.

Writing plays

Born in Cebu City, Linda Kalayaan Faigao-Hall (1948–) moved to the US in 1973, eventually took up graduate studies in English at New York University (NYU) and, later, educational theater at Bretton Hall College, England. She said she became involved in playwriting partly because her father Cornelio was a fiction writer, poet, and journalist. "It seems there was no choice," she said. "It's in my blood. I was exposed to literature in English and Pilipino when I was growing up. I grew up appreciating Jose Garcia Villa and Charles Dickens."

She was briefly involved with Philippine Educational Theatre Arts League in the '70s doing backstage work. The first theater agents she approached turned her down. "They said they could never sell plays about Filipinos," she recalled. "I foolishly proceeded to write my first play. It wasn't even a musical, it had no dancing girls, and nobody sang. It was about a Filipina immigrant and her abortion." "State without Grace" was staged by Pan Asian Repertory Theatre in 1984, then by AATC the following year directed by Dom Magwili.

Faigao-Hall continues to write plays and has been produced across the country, with some works premiered in New York by Ma-Yi Theater in the 1990s and Diverse City Theater in the 2000s. In 2012, she added and has since subsidized the acting and playwriting component of the Cornelio Faigao Memorial Annual Writer's Workshop in Cebu City. She teaches the playwriting component as well, where participants use either English or Cebuano. She published an anthology of her works, "The Female Heart and Other Plays" in 2013.

*

Concerned that plays with ethnic subject matter would be difficult to produce, Jeannie Barroga's (1949–) first two plays, "The Pigeon Man" (1979), which she wrote to cope with her father's death, and "Reaching for the Stars" ('83), featured white characters.

Barroga received a suggestion from Judith Abend, the director of her second play, to write about her own culture. Born and raised in Milwaukee, Barroga thought of her upbringing—as part of the only Filipino family in an all-white community in the Midwest—and wondered how anyone would be interested in a scenario like that. However, upon realizing the inherent humor in the premise, she finally connected her culture with the potential for the stage, but it took a few years before she finally wrote a play with Filipino American characters.

In 1983, she founded Playwright Forum in Palo Alto to help nurture new works. Then in '85, she saw her first theater production that had Asian American actors: Faigo-Hall's "State without Grace" by AATC.

"All of a sudden, doors opened for me. She was a Filipino playwright, it was a Filipino story, there were Filipino actors. It gave me a whole new insight into the possibilities," she said.

Her "Eye of the Coconut," about a Filipino American family's assimilation in Milwaukee, was premiered in '87 by Northwest Asian American Theatre. It was positively received by audiences in Seattle, and later in San Francisco and Los Angeles.

Barroga already has more than 50 plays under her belt and continues to write. Playwright Forum was renamed Discovery Project when it merged in 1986 with the theater company TheaterWorks, where Barroga served as literary manager for more than 15 years.

Some of her works that incorporate Filipino American characters or themes include "Kenny Was A Shortstop" ('91), about gang violence; "Talk Story" ('92), about a Filipino American female journalist's attempt to establish her identity by reliving her father's past; and "Rita's Resources" ('95), a comedy set in the '70s where a Filipino American seamstress' domestic life is interrupted by a visiting sailor.

Some of her plays that touch on history include "Walls" ('88), which deals with the controversy surrounding the Vietnam Memorial in Washington, DC; and "Buffalo'ed" (2012), about David Fagen, one of the African American soldiers who fought in the Philippine-American War and defected to the Philippine side.

Spreading seeds

Though Ferdinand Marcos ended martial law in 1981, the assassination of his political rival Benigno "Ninoy" Aquino, Jr. in 1983 led to increased civic unrest and further loss of confidence in his government. In 1986, presidential elections were held with Aquino's widow Corazon running against him. News of widespread cheating in favor of Marcos triggered mass street demonstrations in civil support for rebel military officers. Protesters formed human blockades against the tanks of government forces as civilians advanced with rebel soldiers to take government strongholds. The Marcos family fled to Hawaii in exile and Corazon "Cory" Aquino was declared the new president. For its relative lack of violence and bloodshed, the event became known as the People Power Revolution.

In the same way the imposition of martial law in the Philippines in the '70s prompted Filipino theater activity in the US, so did the deposing of the dictator. In 1984, cultural arts group Teatro Pilipino was established by spouses Elvi and Rey Bangit, Elvie and Jonathan "Jon" Melegrito, Boots and Gerry Jumat; and Gabby Lopez in Washington, DC to promote Philippine culture and heritage through music and dance performances with the goal of connecting Filipino Americans to their roots. Though its inaugural production was a dance piece depicting the life and work of Ninoy Aquino, the group went on to stage musicals and self-described "folkloric drama" pieces for some time in the late 1980s.

The group later changed its name to Tanghalang Pilipino ng DC [Pilipino Theater of DC] and produced the musical "EDSA!" in 1987 to celebrate the first anniversary of the People Power Revolution. With music and lyrics by George Brooks and Luis Antonio "Chito" Tagle, the musical's title is the acronym of Metro Manila's main thoroughfare, Epifanio de los Santos Avenue, where the revolution's protests were held. The group went on to stage shows such as "Butil-Buhay" ["Grain-Life"] ('87) and "Ito Ang Pilipino" ["This is The Pilipino"] ('88), both written and directed by Nicholas Sengson; and the collaboratively written piece "Bayan Ko, Bumangon Ka" ["My Country, Rise"] in '88.

Miguel Braganza (1960–) served as artistic director for a few years. Born in Davao City, Braganza was already working as a dancer and choreographer in Manila when he moved to the US in '83 to take additional studies in dance at Alvin

Ailey American Dance Center and then at Harvard University in '87, both on scholarships. After his stint with Tanghalang Pilipino ng DC, Braganza went on to act in various "Miss Saigon" productions.

*

In 1986, partly to celebrate the People Power Revolution, Philippine Educational Theater Association (PETA) staged "Panata sa Kalayaan" ["Oath to Freedom"] at the Cultural Center of the Philippines (CCP) and proceeded to produce an English-translation world tour. Chris Millado (1961–) devised, directed, and co-wrote the show using excerpts from existing plays by Filipino playwrights to depict the past and ongoing struggles of different sectors of Philippine society.

Millado had founded activist street theater group Tropang Bodabil [Bodabil Troupe] in 1980 in Manila (renamed Peryante [Carnival Players] in '83), using "political vaudeville" to explore national issues.[38] In '86, he was appointed deputy director for training of the CCP's Outreach and Exchange Division.

He accompanied the tour from September '86 to August '87 across the US. "The tour was significant in the way that it consolidated the audiences developed by Sining Bayan [in the '70s] and planted the seeds for the organization of future Filipino American theater companies," Millado noted. The show also toured the Kennedy Theater in Hawaii in '88. "The experience fired my initiative to pursue work with Filipino American communities in the US," he said.

---

[38] Burns, Lucy. "Theater in the Streets." Our Own Voice Literary Ezine website: Oovrag.com. July 2002. http://oovrag.com/essays/essay2002b-6.shtml

Luz de Leon (1946–), who was based in San Francisco at the time, had been approached by PETA to coordinate the tour. To this end, she established Likha Promotions [Create Promotions] to manage the logistics (not be confused with Likha Pilipino Folk Ensemble [Create Pilipino Folk Ensemble], a dance group that was formed in 1992, also in San Francisco).

After the tour ended, "She sent me to teach theater workshops starting in San Francisco, then to Seattle, Chicago, Washington, DC, and New York," said Millado. "This is how I reconnected with former PETA colleague Angela Mascarenas (who had cofounded Pintig Cultural Group), and former Tropang Bodabil member Ralph Peña (who had cofounded Ma-Yi Theater)."

Shortly after becoming PETA's artistic director in 1990, Millado took up a master's in performance studies at NYU from '91 to '93 and continued to work with Ma-Yi and Pintig during those years before returning to the Philippines where he eventually became artistic director of the CCP.

He also wrote several plays that deal with the American occupation of the Philippines and certain aspects of Filipino American history, including "scenes from an unfinished country 1905/1995," about a Filipino American theater troupe rehearsing a seditious play; "peregriNasyon" ["Wandering Nation"], about Filipino immigrant laborers in the US; and "Nikimalika," about the Igorot who were exhibited at the 1904 World's Fair. These plays were premiered in the US by groups such as Ma-Yi and Pintig.

Because of his involvement in helping set up several

Filipino American theater companies, he is usually described by Filipino American theater makers as the Filipino Johnny Appleseed of Filipino American theater.

National Asian American Theatre Company in New York

Maria Corazon "Mia" Katigbak did not jump at the chance to form the National Asian American Theatre Company (NAATCO) in 1988 when cofounder Chinese American actor Richard Eng pitched the idea to her. She had already been acting with Pan Asian Repertory Theatre and had seen how difficult it can be to run a company.

"But after Richard agreed that the primary focus of the company would be European and American classics with all-Asian American casts, I came on board," she said. "I was increasingly frustrated with the lack of opportunities for acting in the classical canon for trained actors who are Asian American, like me."

Katigbak, who serves as the company's artistic director, said, "We don't get to do these kinds of roles! If doing these roles becomes the foundation of the company, so that we get perceived as technically skilled, then there will have to come a time when people will say, 'Oh right, we don't have to just cast them as Asian gangsters and gooks.'

"I wanted to develop a very large pool of acting talent so that it becomes undeniable that we can do this stuff, and hopefully other people would start casting these folks from our shows." As such, the group aims to "more accurately represent onstage the multi- and intercultural dynamics of our society and demonstrate a rich tapestry of cultural difference bound by the American experience."

Born in Manila, Katigbak and her parents moved to the US when she was 11 years old. "I recall wanting to do theater since I was about five years old," she said. "I was surrounded by musicians and dancers in Manila because my mother, Adelaida Reyes, was a musician and then a music critic [for Philippine Evening News and Manila Daily Bulletin], but theater was always, somehow, in my DNA. There was no 'Aha!' moment, I was just always doing it."[39]

Katigbak said that part of NAATCO's mission is "to increase awareness among non-Asian Americans about our contributions to American culture," and also to point out what "Asian" means. "We can go as far east as Japan, as south as Indonesia, and all the way west to Turkey."

Every season, the company produces an American classic with an all-Asian American cast; an adaptation of a Western classic by an Asian American playwright; and a new work not by, for, or about Asians realized by an all-Asian American cast.

Teatro ng Tanan in San Francisco
In 1988, Luz de Leon saw a group of students performing at a Pilipino Cultural Night at UC Berkeley and invited them to undergo a theater workshop under Chris Millado.

The workshop was conducted in 1989 and the participants

---

[39] Ang. "Obie-winning Mia Katigbak pushes for more Asian faces on the American stage." *PDI*. Aug. 15, 2015.

became the founding members of Teatro ng Tanan [Theater for Everyone]: Mara Torres, who served as the coordinator, and her sibling Alex, Julia Camagong (a former Tropang Bodabil member), Edgar Aguinaldo, and siblings Marlette and Marnelle Marasigan.

The acronym of the group's name, TnT, is a play on the Filipino slang for illegal or undocumented Filipinos abroad. The slang's pun changes the explosive material TNT's letters to stand for "*tago nang tago*," Tagalog for "always hiding (from the authorities)."

"We wanted to change 'tago' to 'tanan'—for Filipino stories to come out of hiding for everyone to see," said Marnelle "Bingo" Marasigan (1970–), who had previously trained in PETA's children's theater workshops before moving to the US in '87 (her older sibling Marlette had trained in the teen theater program).

Stories shared by the participants at the initial workshop were fashioned into the play "Kin: Kamag-Anak." ["Kamag-anak" is Tagalog for "kin."] Set in San Francisco, the play features the stories of a newly arrived immigrant Filipino woman and a young Filipino American man in search of his cultural roots.

After the play was staged as a work-in-progress, the group then approached local playwrights, writers, and poets Jeannie Barroga, Mars Estrada, Oscar Peñaranda, Luis Syquia, and Presco Tabios to help them develop the material further.

"They had a skeletal play which they had been performing,"

explained Barroga. "Our meetings hashed out ideas, and I went off to make them into scenes. When we had our first read-through, we were in tears, all of us blown away by what the actors under Chris came back with."

"The role of Chris Millado cannot be over-emphasized," said De Leon. "He was the guiding light and artistic mover. He infused vitality and strong commitment to the craft." After "Kin," De Leon coordinated other workshops with Filipino American groups in different cities for Millado to conduct.

She then dissolved Likha Promotions and shifted to handling TnT's administrative duties. Before setting up an office in San Francisco, the group's initial base of operations was at the Daly City residence of Violeta "Bullet" Marasigan (the Marasigan siblings' mother), a martial law-era activist.

The members took on varied roles within the group and worked with different directors for their productions. Marnelle, who became company manager for some time, said, "We were all just individuals from the community having fun while learning and doing theater and arts. We got different people based on their strengths, even if they didn't know anything about theater. If you were an accountant, then you did the bookkeeping. If you were a relative or a friend, then you helped carry things around. Whatever needed to be done, people rose to the occasion or position."

"Kin" continued to go through developmental revisions and different stagings until '91. TnT went on to stage other works that focused on immigrant experiences such as Edgar Poma's "Little Train" ('93), about a Filipino American couple preparing to bring their parents to a nursing home; and "Panunuluyan" ["Seeking Shelter"] ('94, annually onward), an adaptation of the devotional Christmas Eve procession dramatizing Catholic icons Mary and Joseph's search for an inn—adapted so that the possible lodgings represented different marginalized Filipino American communities.

"At that time, no one was staging Filipino American plays, much less about the immigrant experience," said Marasigan. "It was about our stories, writing them together, creating them together. It really was a community-building effort. We used what resources we had to empower the community. We really wanted to use theater as a tool for social transformation and change."

Aside from staging productions, the group conducted its Basic Integrated Theater Arts Workshop—which it adapted from PETA's pedagogy—for youth, college students, and cultural workers.

The members also underwent workshops or collaborated with different artists and groups in the Bay Area, such as learning and creating dance pieces under choreographer and dancer Alleluia Panis. Panis moved to the US in the '60s, was a member of dance group Bagong Diwa [New Essence] in the '70s, then of San Francisco Kulintang Ensemble in the early '80s, before striking out on her own as well as reconfiguring the latter group into Kulintang Arts in '86. [Kulintang are knobbed metal gong-chimes.]

The group's other collaborations included studying mime with the San Francisco Mime Troupe through Ron Muriera and staging co-productions of "Kin" with El Teatro Campesino through Ann Fajilan and with TheaterWorks through Barroga.

TnT also collaborated with the Yerba Buena Center for the Arts, which resulted in one landmark project: while not on the scale of a world's fair, 90 years after the St. Louis exhibition, De Leon and TnT helped spearhead the first Filipino American Arts Exposition (FAAE) in 1994. "We linked the 'new' with the buried, undiscovered past," said de Leon.

The event featured exhibits of *kalesa* (horse-drawn carriage), *vinta* (a type of sailboat common to the southern region of the Philippines) and *jeepneys* (public commuter jeeps descended from reconfigured WWII American Army jeeps). It also had a gong ensemble, performers singing *kundiman* (Filipino love ballads), jazz and hip hop music, demonstrations of *tinikling* (a Filipino folk dance where dancers quickly weave in and out of moving bamboo poles), among other performances. During the exposition, TnT also staged Millado's "peregriNasyon."[40]

De Leon left TnT to manage the FAAE (later renamed Filipino Arts And Events) and continued to organize its annual expositions and festivals, later called Pistahan [Fiestas], until she moved back to the Philippines in 2007. FAAE continues to produce Pistahan parades and festivals annually.

"Ate [Elder sister] Luz was the visionary for TnT and the

---

[40] Millado, Chris. "Wandering Stages, Wondering Nations: Postcoloniality and Performance in Philippine Diaspora." Unpublished essay. 1998.

Pistahan," said Marasigan. "If not for her vision and tenacity, the seeds for the Filipino American theater experience would not have been planted."

Ma-Yi Theater in New York
Born in Manila, Ralph Peña (1962–) took a summer workshop with PETA when he was in high school. While a student at UP, he joined Tropang Bodabil and performed at protest rallies against martial law during the early '80s. After he'd been called in for questioning by the military, he left for the US in '84.

He later moved to New York and reconnected with other theater artists from Manila. In 1989, he became a founding member of Ma-Yi Theater, along with Margot Abuan, Luz de Leon (who had briefly left TnT for a few months to work in New York), Anky Frilles, Isolda Oca, Arianne Recto, Cristina Sison, Bernie Villanueva, and Chito Jao Garces, who was founding artistic director. "Ma-Yi" is the ancient Chinese name for pre-Spanish colonial Philippines.

Jorge Ortoll, a former actor with Repertory Philippines, later joined the group to handle the finances. Peña became artistic director in '95 after Garces relocated to another state.

While initially staging works by Filipino playwrights, the group soon moved toward works with Filipino American themes such as Louella Dizon's "Till Voices Wake Us" in '94, about a Filipino American family with clairvoyant women.

Ma-Yi's staging of Peña's "Flipzoids" in '96—about a female

Filipino nurse, her mother, and a male US-born Filipino American, all struggling to reconcile their respective identities—put the company in the spotlight. The title combines "flip," a pejorative for Filipino Americans, and "schizoid," connoting multiple personalities; encapsulating the play's theme of identity.

"It caught the New York theater community by surprise," Peña said. "Before 'Flipzoids,' we struggled to get mainstream press coverage of our works. It was our first production to receive major attention. It helped that the production was directed by Loy Arcenas since he already had a reputation in Broadway circles for his work as a set designer."

But also, that Peña's work obviously resonated with audiences. "I wanted to say something about the Filipino American experience, of how we transact the personal and political acts of locating ourselves in the American landscape. The Filipino community embraced the play immediately, laughing riotously at seeing their own experience on stage.

"I wrote what I knew then, based on observations and my own experiences, and the play triangulated itself between three distinct character tracks: Aying, the new immigrant longing for home; Vangie, the partially assimilated new American reinventing herself; and Redford, a second-generation Filipino American raised with little knowledge of his heritage," he said.

"These three characters tugged at my own understanding of the immigrant experience. It took me over two years to distill the text into what was eventually produced. The play started with 16 characters!" The original cast included Ching Valdes-Aran (Aying) and Mia Katigbak (Vangie). The play has gone on to be staged across the US.

Ma-Yi's increased stature helped it to qualify for grants to sustain its operations. Due to its low ticket prices, the company is sometimes mistaken for an Off-Off-Broadway group. "We're actually an Off-Broadway group because we pay Equity's scale, which is what determines if you have one or two 'Off's. Our pricing is deliberate. We've made a conscious effort to keep our prices affordable for most New Yorkers, but especially for students and seniors." In 1998, the company expanded its focus into an Asian American theater company.[41]

Backstage disciplines

Stage management

Cristina Sison came into stage management by way of acting. She had already completed a basic acting workshop at the Cultural Center of the Philippines in '85. To get free tuition for an advanced acting workshop, she volunteered to assist in a stage management workshop. The lessons she learned in that class inspired her to shift gears.

Upon moving to New York in '89, she became a founding member of Ma-Yi and served as its stage manager. "We went to our respective nine-to-five jobs during the day and did our theater at night," she said. "We were poor but passionate. Our love for theater endured."

---

[41] Ang. "Celebrated Fil-Am play to be restaged in New York." *PDI*. Jan. 17, 2011.

Sison recalled that it was difficult to find actors who could speak Tagalog for the company's initial slew of Filipino plays such as Millado's "Buwan at Baril sa EB Major" ["Moon and Gun in EB Major"].

"So that didn't last long," she said. "Eventually, we did plays written by Filipino playwrights but spoken in English. Then we expanded into plays that dealt with the Asian American experience." Sison eventually joined The Juilliard School as a stage manager.

Music composition and sound design
Fabian Obispo was born and raised in Tayabas City, Quezon province and moved to the US in '74. "Growing up, I was surrounded with music, so it came as no surprise that I played the piano at the age of three-and-a-half without outside help." He studied composition at UP and became the resident composer of the UP Madrigal Singers choir.

"In 1990, Arena Stage in Washington, DC was auditioning composers for their 50th anniversary to compose the music for Bertolt Brecht's 'Caucasian Chalk Circle.' Loy Arcenas submitted my name. I got the job after one interview," said Obispo. "It was a daunting project, especially for someone who did not have any theater experience. In fact, many in the staff did not think I was right for the job but I proved them wrong when I got a glowing review in the New York Times."

With credits such as Ma-Yi's "Flipzoids" and "Romance of Magno Rubio," Obispo has since been composing music and doing sound design for Off-Broadway and regional theater productions across the US.

Costume and set design
Eduardo "Toto" Sicangco (1954–), born in Bacolod, Negros Occidental province, moved to the US in '76 to take up graduate studies in stage design at NYU's Tisch School of the Arts, where he received the Seidman Award for Excellence in Design; and later on, for a degree in Master Teacher of Design. He has since designed costumes and sets for theater and opera productions across the US as well as for film. Some of his work is featured in Lynn Pecktal's 1999 book "Costume Design: Techniques of Modern Masters."

*

Loy Arcenas (1953–), born and raised in Cebu, was a stage manager for the Manila Symphony Society before studying design at the English National Opera in London. He moved to New York in '78 to work with the Third World Institute of Theatre Arts Studies at La MaMa Experimental Theatre Club (La MaMa), and to train under Sicangco.

In addition to his work with Ma-Yi and other Off-Broadway groups, he has designed the sets for Broadway productions of "Prelude to a Kiss" ('90), "Once on This Island" ('90), "The Glass Menagerie" ('94), and "The Night of the Iguana" ('96), among others. He received an Obie Award for Sustained Excellence of Set Design in '93. Arcenas eventually shifted to directing and filmmaking.

In 1997, Arcenas was involved in a court case that set a precedent for set designs to be copyrightable. He was first alerted to a plagiarism incident when an actor friend informed him that his set design for the '94 Broadway production of "Love! Valour! Compassion!" had been copied by Caldwell Playhouse (later Theatre Company) in Boca

Raton, Florida. "Caldwell had copied all the production design elements. My design for 'Love! Valour! Compassion!' was one of a kind," Arcenas said.

"I did not base my designs on anything that Terrence McNally described in the set requirements as written in his published version of the script. I designed a green landscape, something sensual, on which the many goings-on in the play happened. It was so different from the many moveable spaces Terrence had envisioned."

United Scenic Artists, the union for set designers, arranged for a lawyer to work with Arcenas. First, to file for a copyright for his design, then to file a lawsuit against Caldwell Playhouse. Caldwell Playhouse then filed a motion to have the case dismissed, though US District Judge Kenneth Ryskamp, who referred to the suit as the "Case of the Stolen Stage Designs," denied the motion.

Arcenas recalled, "A number of designers were not supportive of the suit at that time. 'Why rock the boat?' some asked. But it went smoothly and I won my case." A settlement was reached and Caldwell Playhouse paid Arcenas an amount he would have received if he had designed the set for them; he donated a portion of his fee to the union's Sick and Benefit Fund. United Scenic Artists' website noted that the favorable ruling was considered a landmark legal decision.[42]

*

Robert Brill, whose mother is Filipino, was born in Salinas,

---

[42] Goodman, David. "Love! Valour! Compassion!" United Scenic Artists Local USA 829 website: Usa829.org. 2000. http://Usa829.org.

California and studied theater at UC San Diego, during which he became a cofounder of Sledgehammer Theatre (1984). He was first drawn to puppetry and magic as a child before transitioning to set design. He has designed sets for theater and opera across the US. His designs have graced the stages of Center Theatre Group, La Jolla Playhouse, Old Globe Theatre, Goodman Theatre, and the Oregon Shakespeare Festival, among others.

His Broadway credits include "One Flew Over the Cuckoo's Nest" (2001), "Assassins" (2004), "A Streetcar Named Desire" (2005), and "Guys and Dolls" (2009), among others. In 2004, he received the Michael Merritt Award for Excellence in Design and Collaboration.

CIRCA-Pintig in Chicago
Angela Mascarenas had trained with PETA throughout her childhood. "I started with their summer teen theater workshop way back in 1976," she said. She moved to Chicago in '83 and joined anti-Marcos activist group Philippine Forum. She recommended that the group use performances as an education tool. "My co-members in the youth committee and I decided to focus on doing cultural organizing and started our own group in 1986."[43]

In 1991, they renamed their organization to Pintig Cultural Group [Pulse Cultural Group]. Mascarenas found out that Chris Millado was studying in New York at the time and asked him to conduct workshops for the group. "He

---

[43] Ang. "Chicago's Circa Pintig theater group gets set for 25th year." *Inquirer.net.* Nov. 28, 2015. http://globalnation.inquirer.net/132897/chicagos-circa-pintig-theater-group-gets-set-for-25th-year

basically trained us in all aspects of production, both onstage and backstage, and in engaging the wider community with our work," she said.

"He was a wonderful and masterful mentor to all of us. I don't think Pintig would be around without Chris. He's essentially one of the founders of Pintig." The group's inaugural production was Millado's play "America is in the Heart," adapted from Carlos Bulosan's novel and directed by Millado in '92.

Other core founding members and volunteers include Levi Aliposa, Rey Belen, Riza Belen, Divina Calo, Daisy Castro, Jerry Clarito, Susan Gonzalez-Kirpach, Ginger Leopoldo, Ramon Mascarenas, Edessa Ramos, Jimi Reyes, and Allan Sargan.

Mascarenas also credited Filipino playwright Rodolfo "Rody" Vera as a helpful contributor to the group's early years. The group staged several of his works such as "Alamat" ["Legends"], about the exhibited Igorot at St. Louis.

The group also staged Vera's "Bells of Balangiga" ('97), with music composed by Louie Pascasio. The musical is about how, on September 28, 1901, in the town of Balangiga, Eastern Samar province, Filipinos—upon being signaled by ringing church bells—launched a surprise attack against American soldiers. In retaliation, Brigadier General Jacob Smith ordered all Filipinos 10 years and older to be killed. In 1904, the American soldiers took three of the church bells to the US.

In 2001, Pintig members formed the Center for Immigrant

Resources and Community Arts (CIRCA) to focus on activities for their children. "Several of us had children who were growing up and we wanted to provide a safe and creative space for them so that they could learn their Filipino history and culture, and get more involved with the Filipino community in Chicago. So essentially, CIRCA was for youths while Pintig was for adults. It became one entity with Pintig in 2006."

Mascarenas noted that the group's thrust is not just training performers, but also, as drawn from the pedagogy developed by PETA, molding artists-teachers/trainers-organizers-researchers, or what the group terms as "ators."

"Very often, we have individuals who come to our events seeking to be trained as professional actors. Our usual response is, if that is all they want, then they will be better served in other theater groups," she said.

The group immerses its volunteers and students in using theater as a tool in tackling community issues. Mascarenas said CIRCA-Pintig deals with issues such as internalized racism, homophobia, economic exploitation, and youth trafficking—in creative and engaging ways.

"CIRCA-Pintig prides itself on being distinct in the sense that we do not exist simply for entertainment or doing art for art's sake. We are a theater group that engages community members in collective action through the arts. We strive to produce professionally done performances without sacrificing the values and principles of collective empowerment and self-determination."

The Filipino connection of "Miss Saigon"

The musical "Miss Saigon" opened on Broadway on April 11, 1991—produced by Cameron Mackintosh (British) with music by Claude-Michel Schonberg (French) and English lyrics by Richard Maltby, Jr. (white American) adapted from the original French lyrics by Alain Boublil (French). Based on opera composer Giacomo Puccini's "Madama Butterfly" (1904), the musical is set during the Vietnam War where Vietnamese Kim falls in love with and is abandoned by a white American GI. When they reunite years later, she kills herself to force him to take their son with him back to the United States.

The show had its world premiere in London in '89. For that production, the producers had held auditions in New York, Hollywood, and Hawaii but could not find the actors they needed for key roles. It was in Manila where they found actors, several of whom had trained with Repertory Philippines, to fill their cast.

The West End production's two leads received Laurence Olivier Awards: Best Actor in a Musical for Welsh actor Jonathan Pryce as the pimp Engineer and Best Actress in a Musical for Filipino actor Lea Salonga as Kim.

Mackintosh wanted the London leads to play on Broadway as well. Asian American theater artists complained to Equity about the casting of Pryce in an ostensibly Eurasian role and about being denied the opportunity to audition for the role. Protests were also made against the show's negative stereotypes of Asians, such as women being submissive and overly-sexualized.

After threatening to pull out the show, Mackintosh prevailed. The show already had the biggest advance ticket sales in Broadway history at the time and would be employing close to 30 Asian American actors. Equity also initially turned down his request to include Salonga in the cast but reversed its decision after he demanded arbitration.[44]

In 1991, for her work in "Miss Saigon," Lea Salonga (1971–) became the first Filipino woman to receive a Tony Award— for the Best Actress in a Musical category. Salonga had acted in English-language musicals and plays as a child with Repertory Philippines and had already been working as a recording artist and a television and film actor in her teens before her West End and Broadway debuts. She returned several times to reprise the Kim role during the show's run, including in 2001 to close the run.

Her involvement in this musical established a career that has inspired many theater actors, Filipino Americans or otherwise. Salonga has since returned to the US several times to perform in other Broadway productions, including "Les Miserables" as Eponine in 1993 during its original run and then Fantine in 2007 during its revival run; and "Flower Drum Song" as Mei Li in a 2002 revival that used a new script by David Henry Hwang.

Even without counting international productions, the multiple productions of "Miss Saigon" in the US alone (in addition to the Broadway run, there have been national tours and regional productions) have provided acting

---

[44] Gerard, Jeremy. "The Verdict's In and Salonga's B'way Bound." *Variety*. Jan. 13, 1991.

opportunities for many Filipino American actors. The Kim role and several ensemble parts have usually been cast with Filipino American actors.

After Pryce, the Engineer role has since always been cast with actors of Asian heritage—usually Filipino Americans. The first to be cast was Chinese Filipino actor Francis Ruivivar (1960–2001), who was born in Hong Kong, raised in Hawaii, and made his Broadway debut in "Chess" in '88. He filled in when Pryce was on vacation and eventually took over the role.

Families have been created through the show and generations of families have been in the show. Deedee Magno (1975–), born in Portsmouth, Virginia, played Kim in the second national tour in '95 and met her spouse Cliffton Hall, who was in the ensemble, in the show. Magno-Hall went on to play Kim on Broadway, and Nessarose in the national tour of "Wicked" (2006-08), among others.

Annette Calud (1963–), born in Milwaukee, was in the ensemble and a Kim understudy in the Broadway premiere and eventually replaced Salonga in '92. Her paternal cousin's daughter, San Diego-native Eva Noblezada (1996–), was cast as Kim for the 2014-16 West End revival and will reprise the role for the 2017-18 Broadway revival.

Calud, who eventually worked in television, used to accompany Noblezada when she was a child to watch Broadway shows.[45] "I took her to see 'Beauty and the Beast,' 'The Lion King,' and 'Phantom of the Opera.' I was fortunate

---

[45] Ang. "Fil-Am Eva Noblezada is new 'Miss Saigon' on West End." *PDI*. Nov. 23, 2013.

to get to work through the songs with her before she auditioned," said Calud. "Though she didn't need much help at all. Hearing her sing, I knew for certain she would land the part."

Playwrights' Arena in Los Angeles

When Jon Lawrence Rivera (1960–) founded Playwrights' Arena in 1992, the Rodney King riots erupted after the theater company's first show opened in Hollywood. The days-long riots were incited by the acquittal of white police officers who had been on trial for using excessive force when they arrested King, who is African American.

That's when Rivera decided to devote the company to staging new plays by Los Angeles playwrights. "People had no place to put their energies," Rivera had said in a previous interview. "I knew I could promote local playwrights who'd been complaining that no one produced them unless they've been successful somewhere else."

Born in Manila, Rivera and his family left the Philippines after his journalist father Jose Lorenzo "Larry" Rivera was blacklisted by the Marcos dictatorship. Australia granted them asylum, and Rivera studied acting in Sydney before relocating to the US in '79, where he eventually studied film directing at Los Angeles City College.

After he worked as a freelance director and producer, a desire to work on material that he would be personally passionate about prompted him and an actor friend to rent a theater and put on a play. The company now stages two to four productions a year by playwrights of all colors, all world premieres or Los Angeles premieres. It also has a staged reading series for new works in development.

It has not been without challenges. Rivera's commitment to premiering new works instead of staging more commercial fare is one of the reasons why his founding partner departed. Rivera's insistence on diversity on stage has cost him projects. "There's a resistance to it, mostly by white producers, because it's not a world they see, or they refuse to see, even though it's in front of them every day."[46]

Writing more plays

Born in Manila, Han Ong (1968–) moved to Los Angeles with his family in 1984. He took a drama course in high school and was then accepted to a young playwright's lab at Los Angeles Theater Center. In '91, his "Symposium in Manila," a monologue which he also performed himself, was staged at Highways Performance Space in Santa Monica, California and at The Public Theater (The Public) in New York.

Ong gained notice in the industry after Boston's American Repertory Theater (ART) artistic director Robert Brustein praised his work. He had three works staged the following year: "Cornerstone Geography," another solo piece; "Bachelor Rat;" and "Reasons to Live. Reason to Live. Half. No Reason"—the last two of which ran simultaneously in the San Francisco Bay Area with another run of "Symposium." All while his "The LA Plays," comprised of one-acts "In a Lonely Country" and "A Short List of Alternate

---

[46] Ang. "LA director soldiers on to boost new voices." *Inquirer.net*. Mar. 2, 2017. http://usa.inquirer.net/1911/la-playwright-director-soldiers-boost-new-voices

Places," was being developed by ART for a '93 production (which eventually also had a London staging the same year).

In 1993, he wrote "Swoony Planet," where Filipino American Jessica helps an Indian woman search for her runaway son while Jessica's own son searches for his estranged father. He also collaborated with Jessica Hagedorn on performance piece "Airport Music," which the pair performed that year and again in '94. He moved to New York in '94 and continues to write plays and novels.

In 1997, he received a MacArthur Fellowship, popularly known as the "Genius" grant, awarded to individuals who "have shown extraordinary originality and dedication in their creative pursuits and a marked capacity for self-direction." Some of his other works with Filipino American themes include "Middle Finger," an adaptation of Frank Wedekind's "Spring Awakening" with Filipino American students at a Catholic school. It was premiered by Ma-Yi Theater in New York in 2000.

*

In 1994, Nicky Paraiso (1951–) began his trilogy of autobiographical multimedia one-person plays. Beginning with "Asian Boys" (co-produced with Ma-Yi) and followed by "Houses and Jewels," both about growing up gay and Filipino in Queens. The trilogy concluded a decade later in 2004 with "House/Boy," recollections of his visits in the 1980s to his mother back in the Philippines. For his shows, Paraiso combined confessional monologues, singing, dancing, acting, and projections in a cabaret-like performance.

After studying theater and piano performance at Oberlin College and a master's in acting at NYU, Paraiso has been active in the theater industry since '79; has been a member of Meredith Monk and Vocal Ensemble, and The House throughout the '80s, touring extensively throughout the US, Europe, and Japan; and has worked with other experimental theater artists. He later assumed administrative positions at La MaMa, and has been its Cultural Minister and Director of Programming since 2001.

*

Jessica Tarahata Hagedorn (1949–) has been a multidisciplinary artist since the '70s, though it was her 1998 play "Dogeaters" that helped generate attention for her work in mainstream theater. Born in Manila to parents of mixed Filipino, Asian, and European heritage, Hagedorn settled in San Francisco in '63. In the '70s, she wrote poetry, took acting lessons at American Conservatory Theater, and founded rock band The Gangster Choir ('75–'85), a group that mixed music and poetry. She moved to New York in '78 and began staging one-person multimedia performance art pieces at The Public such as "Mango Tango" and "Tenement Lover," using song, poetry, images, and spoken dialogue.

She then shifted to writing, with her first novel "Dogeaters" debuting in 1990, a sprawling account of Filipino characters living under a dictator regime. The book attracted attention for receiving the American Book Award that year and also because of its controversial title, considered a pejorative for Filipinos.

She wrote a one-act play, "Surrender," based on a chapter from the book that was staged by Ma-Yi in '91. Director

Michael Greif, whom she had met when both were artistic associates at The Public, asked if she'd be interested in adapting her entire book into a play. After a workshop at Sundance Theater Laboratory in Utah in '97, "Dogeaters" premiered the following year at La Jolla Playhouse, San Diego, where Greif was artistic director at the time.

Hagedorn continues to write novels, edit anthologies, and do theater work. Playwriting credits include the book for the musical "Most Wanted," for La Jolla Playhouse, loosely inspired by the life and crimes of Andrew Cunanan, the Filipino American who murdered fashion designer Gianni Versace.

Staging stories
Sining KilUSAn in Seattle
In 1991, Timoteo "Tim" Cordova (1957–) founded Sining KilUSAn [Art Movement] in Seattle. The group's inaugural production was "Across Oceans of Dreams" ('92), a play he had written when he was 17 years old, about the Filipino immigrant laborers of the '30s, with music by Ramon Salvador and Manuel Carrillo.

"I have always worked in the community. I felt there was a need to create a group," he said. "I saw Pinoys not being able to play strong roles or they'd have to settle for roles outside of their culture, like playing Mexicans or Native Americans, as opposed to playing strong Filipino characters.

"My work in theater is an outgrowth of my work in the community. I wanted to give opportunities to people so that they, in turn, could give opportunities to other people."

Other productions he wrote and directed for the group include "Barkada Syndrome" ('94), about gang violence ["Barkada" is "gang"]; and "Bamboo Split" ('95), about young lovers from different backgrounds. His "Heart of the Son," with music by Damian Cordova, Angelo Pizarro, Ramon Salvador, and Joel Sison, about the Philippine revolution against Spain, was first staged in '96, then in tours in '98 and 2004 as far south as San Diego and as far east as Virginia state.

"When I stage productions, I don't look at the reactions of the Filipinos, I look at the reactions of the non-Filipinos," he said. "Are they taking us seriously? We should be proud of ourselves but it's more important that our counterparts in America respect us. They need to know about us."

Hawaii Alliance for Philippine Performing Arts
in Honolulu

Ana Valdes-Lim (1960–) moved to New York to study theater at The Juilliard School in 1980. She then acted and taught with groups such as John Houseman's The Acting Company and The Public Theater, and performed in cities such as New York, Washington, DC, and Los Angeles.

While studying for a professional diploma in elementary education at University of Hawaii (UH), she acted in and served as acting coach for a touring production of "Kasla Gloria Ti Hawaii" [Ilocano for "Hawaii is Like Paradise"] written and directed by Behn Cervantes.

"It toured the outer islands. I taught improv and voice. At the same time, I was dancing and touring with Pamana Dancers, which was a folk dance group started by Hana

Trinidad," she said. ["Pamana" is Tagalog for "heritage."] (Trinidad had been in the first group of volunteers who joined Bayanihan Dance Company in the late '50s before she moved to Hawaii.)

In 1992, she cofounded Hawaii Alliance for Performing Arts (HAPA) with John Coronel and Neric Acosta, both of whom she had met through the "Kasla" production. "We founded HAPA to provide a platform for artists to produce their own works. Our goals were to create a hub for theater artists. It compelled us to create," she said. The group's inaugural production was a staging of "Lucila Lalu," a play written by Coronel about the titular murder victim in the Philippines in the late '60s.

Valdes-Lim returned to Manila in '94 and established a career as a director and teacher. She went on to found Philippine Playhouse, a theater group that focuses on improvisation, and was appointed by Assumption College in 2004 to found the school's theater group Marie Eugenie Theater of the Assumption. She has also written several books on acting.

Chris Millado worked with HAPA in '95 while he taught at UH and reconfigured the group to stage Filipino American-themed productions. The group renamed itself Hawaii Alliance for Philippine Performing Arts and remained active for a few more years.

Slant in New York
Wayland Quintero (1969–) was born in Sagada, Mountain Province and moved to Hawaii with his family when he was still a baby. He discovered modern dance in college and

later moved to New York in '89 to pursue a master's in dance at NYU's Tisch School of the Arts. He eventually performed with groups such as Ping Chong and Company, Tandy Beal and Company, Gus Solomons Jr. Dance Company, and HT Chen and Dancers. "I then got involved at La MaMa," he said. "They do everything over there. It became my artistic home with my development as a theater artist. When I think of theater, I think of an all-encompassing practice."

His collaborations with other artists led to the cofounding of musical satirical performance group Slant in 1995 with Chinese American Perry Yung and Japanese American Richard Ebihara. The group's inaugural production was "Big Dicks, Asian Men" at La MaMa, about three Asian American men at a police lineup whose alibis become "individual vignettes of theater, choreography, and live music celebration of their most cherished experiences of American upbringing and homage to the guiding influences of their Asian heritage."

Through their work, the group explored culture stereotypes surrounding Asian American masculinity and, later on, also tackled Asian American history and cultural appropriation. The group created nine more original productions that were performed across the US; the group remained active until 2004.

Peeling in New York
In 1995, Los Angeles-native Gary San Angel (1972–) founded Asian American performance group Peeling the Banana in New York, focusing on autobiographical material staged

with poetry, dance, and music. San Angel replicated the process he had been part of the previous year as a participant in Chinese Japanese American Dan Kwong's workshop in Los Angeles—developing the participants' own stories into material for the stage.

The group had its inaugural performance in '96. After directing most of the group's shows for several years, San Angel relocated to Philadelphia in '99 to initiate new groups there. He has since delved into filmmaking and has been an artist-in-residence at the Asian Arts Initiative.

In 2000, after some restructuring, the group elected Dan Bacalzo (1970–) as the new artistic director. He had attended his first Peeling the Banana show in '98 and was invited by performer Regie Cabico to join the group. "I had been touring a solo show 'I'm Sorry, But I Don't Speak the Language,' which I premiered at the first New York International Fringe Festival in '97," Bacalzo recounted. "The piece was autobiographical and primarily looking at my overlapping identities as a gay man and a Filipino American."

The group's name was officially shortened to Peeling. "Partly as a way to mark the shift in membership to include new recruits," he said. Peeling continued to conduct writing and performance workshops that resulted in stagings and stayed active until 2003.

Born in Flushing, New York, Bacalzo took up a doctorate in performance studies at NYU. He eventually started writing about Asian American performance for InTheater Magazine in '99, and later for TheaterMania.com, where he became managing editor until 2012. He has gone on to teach at Florida Gulf Coast University.

Campo Santo in San Francisco

In 1996, writer, performer, and director Sean San Jose, whose mother is Filipino and father is Puerto Rican, cofounded multicultural theater company Campo Santo [Spanish for "Sacred Ground"] in San Francisco with Margo Hall, Luis Saguar, and Michael Torres.

The group takes "the sacred form of storytelling and uses it as a tool to bond community through socially relevant plays." Campo Santo has ongoing collaborations with different playwrights, including Jessica Hagedorn. It has produced her plays "Stairway to Heaven" (2005), where Nena falls in love with a homeless man, and its sequel "Fe in the Desert" (2007), where robbers invade Fe's home.

San Jose also worked with Magic Theatre when he memorialized his mother's death in 1994—due to HIV (human immunodeficiency virus)-related causes—by conceiving "Pieces of the Quilt," a project that collected vignettes from various playwrights about the AIDS (acquired immune deficiency syndrome) epidemic, which premiered in '96 and ran for three years. San Jose had also dropped his father's surname, Blackman, to honor his mother's memory.

He has also worked as program director of arts organization Intersection for the Arts' performance program, overseeing premiere productions of theater, dance, and interdisciplinary performances.

Creating characters

There are many Filipino American actors who have performed and continue to perform across the US. Ching Valdes-Aran and Jose Llana are two actors who gained notice in the mid-'90s in New York City.

Ching Valdes-Aran received an Obie Award for Performance for her work in Ma-Yi's 1996 staging of "Flipzoids." Born in San Nicolas, Ilocos Norte province, she joined Filipinescas Dance Company in Manila when she was 13 years old. She moved to New York in '67 and became the lead dancer and assistant director of the Philippine Dance Company of New York, which was founded by Bruna Pascua Seril in '43.

"I was also a member of Reynaldo Alejandro Dance Theater around the same time. We were both members of the All Nations Dance Company, too," she said. In 1977, she began conceptualizing, choreographing, and directing solo dance pieces, such as "Ilocana."

A show she saw at La MaMa inspired her to shift to acting. "It was all by accident! I never thought I was an actress. Doing text scared me to death. Then I met many downtown artists from all over the world, primarily at La MaMa." That was where she caught a revival production of Andrei Serban's "Greek Trilogy."

"It was electrifying! The performers were hand-picked from all over the world. Elizabeth Swados created made-up, heightened language into songs. It was dance theater at its height. It must have been 1978 or 1979. I thought to myself, 'I can do this. I want to do this!'"

She met several emigrants from the Philippines who had left because of martial law. "Like Cecile Guidote-Alvarez, Bobby Guidote, Melvi Pacubas, Ding Pajaron, Rudy Hermano and many others who were part of PETA and continued their work at La MaMa.

"At the same time, Pan Asian Repertory was then a resident company of La MaMa. There I met many Asian American artists and the few Filipino Americans like Raul Aranas, Mia Katigbak, Ernest Abuba, Jessica Hagedorn, David Henry Hwang.

"That's how I began to become an 'actress.' It took me a while to call myself one," she said. Valdes-Aran has since acted nationwide and internationally. She has essayed leading roles such as Medea, Empress of China, Bernarda Alba, Clytemnestra, Lady Macbeth, and Jocasta, to name a few.

Jose Llana (1976–) technically stole someone else's slot when he auditioned for the 1996 Broadway revival of "The King and I." He had raised his hand when another auditionee did not show up. Llana sang, then promptly confessed. "I was a college freshman, I didn't know better," he said, laughing.

All was forgiven and—just freshly arrived in New York from Washington, DC to study classical voice at Manhattan School of Music—he debuted on Broadway as Lun Tha. (The show's King of Siam was played by film actor Lou Diamond Phillips, who was born in the Philippines to a Filipino mother.)

Born in Manila, Llana relocated to the US with his family when he was three years old. "I consider myself lucky to have seen many touring Broadway productions where I grew up. 'Les Miserables,' 'Cats' and 'Fiddler on the Roof' are some of my favorites. And, of course, I also watched movie musicals like 'West Side Story' and 'Sound of Music.' I was also lucky to have had a top-notch theater and music department in my high school, Thomas Jefferson High School for Science and Technology. My best friends today are still my friends from my high school choir and drama groups."[47]

Llana went on to play Wang Ta opposite Lea Salonga in the Broadway revival of "Flower Drum Song" (2002) and originated the role of Chip Tolentino in the musical "The 25th Annual Putnam County Spelling Bee" (2005), a role that was not originally written with any ethnicity, though he worked with the show's creators to turn the character into a Filipino American.

Other Broadway credits include Angel in "Rent" and El Gato in "Wonderland: Alice's New Musical Adventure." In 2015, Llana was cast as the King of Siam in the Broadway revival of "The King and I," taking over for Japanese film actor Ken Watanabe, who had opened the run, and going on to play the role for the national tour.

Endeavors in Washington, DC
Kilos Sining
In 1987, Kilos Sining [Movement Arts] was founded in

---

[47] Ang. "Jose Llana takes over from Ken Watanabe in 'The King and I' on Broadway." *PDI*. Jul. 25, 2015.

Washington, DC by George Brooks, Nicky Morales, Ellen Payongayong, Teresa Simbulan, Romel Simon, Art Victoria, and Munam Villorante. The group staged Filipino plays in Tagalog until '89 with Villorante, who moved to the US in '75, directing most of its productions.

Nicky's sibling Angelina "Leni" Morales-Encarnacion, who had been a performer with the Bayanihan Dance Company and UP Madrigal Singers back in the Philippines, produced the group's 1989 staging of "Larawan" ["Portrait"], a translation of Joaquin's "A Portrait of the Artist as Filipino."

The production's second staging in New Jersey gave birth to Pintig New Jersey [Pulse New Jersey]. "It evolved to become a community-based cultural group using theater arts, music, and dance," she said.

"I was also involved in the formation of Potri Ranka Manis' (who is from the Maranao people from southern Philippines) dance group Kinding Sindaw in New York." ["Kinding Sindaw" is Maranao for "Dance of Light."]

Bahaghari Productions
Director and actor Sarah Joaquin (1909–2002) founded Far Eastern University (FEU) Drama Guild in Manila in 1934. While schools were still closed after WWII, she worked with Charles Vance, a captain of the US Army, and headed Filipiniana—a roving troupe that entertained troops throughout the Philippines—for a year.

When schools reopened, she resumed duties at FEU Drama Guild (later Theater Guild) and directed for other groups such as the Manila Theatre Guild. In her autobiography "Of

Laughter and Tears" (2007), she recalls how she learned to be punctual while working for the US Army, a trait she later instilled in her students, earning her the nickname "The Terror of FEU." She was able to study theater at Catholic University of America in Washington, DC under a Fulbright scholarship from '61 to '62.

After decades of doing theater work in the Philippines, Joaquin retired to Washington, DC in '77. She became active in theater again in the '90s, acting in or directing plays such as Filomena Colendrino's "Why Women Wash the Dishes" ('93), her brother-in-law Nick Joaquin's "May Day Eve" ('94), and Marcelino Agana's "A New Yorker in Tondo" ('94).

In 1995, Joaquin cofounded Bahaghari Productions [Rainbow Productions] with the aim of showcasing Philippine cultural heritage on the stage, in the vernacular, for the entertainment of the Filipino American community.

Its inaugural production that year was a trilogy of one-acts presented as "Tatluhang Dula" ["Three Plays"]: "Ang Mundo ay Isang Mansanas" ["The World is An Apple"], "Kamatayan ng Isang Duwag" ["Death of a Coward"], and "Panhik Ligaw," D. Habito's translation/adaptation of Anton Chekhov's "The Marriage Proposal." That year, she also directed Servando de los Angeles' sarsuwela "Ang Kiri" ["The Coquette"].

Bahaghari Productions frequently worked with Tanghalang Pilipino ng DC, sharing actors and other resources. The group was active until the late '90s.

QBd Ink

Tanghalang Pilipino ng DC staged the folkloric drama "Hanap Mula" ["Always Searching"] in 1993. With music by Nicholas Sengson and lyrics by Jaime Yambao, the show is about a lost Filipino traveler who must recapture the memory of his country before he can find his way. Remedios "Remy" Cabacungan's (1908–2010) walk-on part was to enter a market with the line, "*Que barbaridad! Ang baho-baho naman dito!*" ["How awful! It stinks here!"].

The line inspired the name of theater group QBd Ink, founded in 1994 by Cabacungan, Bob Caparas, Rod Garcia and Reme-Antonia Grefalda (1941–). The group was initially created to be a production company to provide other theater and dance groups with technical and manpower support such as lighting equipment and stage crew.

It also conducted workshops such as stage management and creative dramatics for children. It eventually attracted a pool of actors and theater workers, and started staging its own productions in '95. Aside from acting, Cabacungan handled production management, marketing, and ticket sales. Her daughter Grefalda served as the group's strategist, resident playwright, and artistic director.

Cabacungan and Grefalda moved to the US from the Philippines in 1960. Grefalda took up English literature at Dickinson University, New Jersey, though she originally pursued journalism at St. Paul College, Manila, where she had been classmates with Cecile Guidote. While visiting Manila in '67, Grefalda became involved with PETA, writing scripts, acting, handling teen theater and creative dramatics for children, and preparing documentation for souvenir programs or playbills. She stayed in Manila for a few years and worked as one of Guidote's right hands in strategy, direction, casting, and production planning. With rampant rumors of impending martial law circulating, Grefalda was summoned back to the US in 1971.

With QBd, Grefalda wrote plays such as "Mama, Mama, Do We Have Rehearsals Tonite?" (a children's musical) and "Who Sez I'm A Coconut?" (a one-person show on the pains and joys of growing up Filipino American). She has also tackled areas of Philippine history with plays such as "30 December 1896," about Filipino writer and doctor Jose Rizal, who is regarded as a national hero against the Spanish colonizers; and "In the Matter of Willie Grayson," about the Philippine-American War. The group stayed active until 2003.

Asian Stories in America
In 1998, Eduardo "Edu." Bernardino cofounded Asian Stories in America (ASIA) in Washington, DC with Korean American actor Stan Kang for a number of reasons: Asian-related works were not being staged in the area, he was not being cast in non-Asian roles, and he wanted to give opportunities to local Asian American actors and other theater artists such as playwrights, designers, and technicians.

Bernardino's family moved to the US in '74 when he was 11 years old. After completing film and television studies in Chicago, he moved to DC in '87, working as an actor and, starting in '96, as a costume designer for Washington Shakespeare Company, among other groups. Filipino American plays that were staged by ASIA include

"Flipzoids" in 2001 and "Middle Finger" for the group's last active year in 2002.

Bindlestiff Studio in San Francisco

A native of Monterey, California, Allan Manalo (1963–) became involved with Pilipino American Collegiate Endeavor while he attended San Francisco State University. Working with the student group gave him opportunities to explore his Filipino roots as well as to cut his teeth in crafting scripts. After he was recruited to write the script for the group's Pilipino Cultural Night, he went on to write and direct the next three annual installments.

After college, he acted for groups such as Asian American Theatre Company and TnT. In 1992, he founded the sketch comedy group tongue in A mood with Kennedy Kabasares, Ron Muriera, and Rex Navarette. The group's irreverent personality is manifested in its name, a phonetic match to the Tagalog curse phrase "*(pu)ta'ng ina mo*" ["your mom's a whore"].

Initially formed upon the invitation of writer Oscar Peñaranda to perform at a Filipino fiesta, the group went on to perform at Holy City Zoo comedy club for about a year before disbanding. Kabasares continued to act and eventually became an aerialist, Muriera went into community engagement and consulting, and Navarette continued with stand-up comedy.

Manalo visited Manila for a month in '95, interacting with activists as well as theater artists from PETA. Upon his return to the US, he embarked on a stand-up show tour in the college circuit. He returned to San Francisco in '97, newly married to theater artist Joyce Juan.[48] Manalo wanted to resurrect tongue in A mood and recruited writers such as Kevin Camia and Patty Cachapero.

As the new group searched for a venue, actor Ogie Gonzales suggested Bindlestiff Studio—the venue where he was playing music for Lorna Aquino Chui's (later Velasco) solo show. When Manalo and Juan went to inspect the studio, despite it being in a rundown neighborhood, he immediately "fell in love with the space."

Bindlestiff was founded in 1989 by Canadian puppeteer and director Chrystene Ells, who used the vacant storefront to put on shows and conduct workshops for neighborhood kids, one of whom had been Aquino Chui.

The name Bindlestiff combines the slang word "bindle," for bundle or a junkie's drug paraphernalia; and the Depression-era term for itinerant laborers or working "stiffs," also known as tramps and hobos.

In September '97, tongue in A mood opened its new show at Bindlestiff. It went on to have successful runs, effectively becoming one of the studio's resident performing companies. The group went on to develop more theatrical ways of presenting shows, such as including movement and shadow-puppetry.

By 1998, TnT also became a resident group at the studio until its dissolution a few years later. Partly because only

---

[48] Pimentel, Benjamin. "Filipino Group Finds Its Own Humor." *San Francisco Chronicle*. Aug. 13, 2000.

the Filipino American productions were having box office success, the studio's management was turned over to Manalo and Juan. The couple went on to reconfigure the studio's programming to focus on Filipino American performing artists.

Since then, Bindlestiff Studio—describing itself as the "Epicenter of Filipino American Performing Arts"—has hosted different resident groups and produced or co-produced original plays, stand-up and sketch comedy shows, concerts, music festivals, etc. The eclectic programming has appealed to the local Filipino American community and has served to provide them with an array of theater forms to experience and explore.

4
Engage
(2000s-2010s)

Developing and guiding

The 2000s saw the proliferation of mobile devices, such as smartphones and tablets, which provided more ways to access the internet. By the 2010s, social media and streaming services have become prevalent channels for communications and entertainment.

Owing to improvements and investments made in the 1990s, Broadway had a renewed popularity and iconic status. On Sept. 11, 2001, the World Trade Center complex in New York City was destroyed by terrorists using hijacked passenger planes, resulting in thousands of deaths and injuries. To serve as a symbol of the city's resilience, the theater industry was tasked to open immediately by Mayor Rudolph Giuliani together with City Hall and the New York

Stock Exchange. Two days later, at a news conference, the mayor addressed the public, "The best thing you can do for our city is take in a Broadway show."

In the 2000s and first half of the 2010s, jukebox musicals (shows that combine existing songs into a cohesive storyline) became popular, such as "Jersey Boys," "Rock of Ages," "American Idiot," "Motown the Musical," and "On Your Feet!"

As Filipino American theater makers continued to engage with the communities they serve, they also continued to gain recognition for their efforts.

In May 2003, Ma-Yi Theater Company's production of "The Romance of Magno Rubio" received Special Citations from the Obie Awards for Lonnie Carter (playwright), Loy Arcenas (director), and the entire cast, which consisted of Arthur Acuña, Ramon de Ocampo, Ron Domingo, Jojo Gonzalez, Orlando Pabotoy, and Ralph Peña. The play has gone on to be staged across the country.

In 2007, the company published "Savage Stage: Plays By Ma-Yi Theater Company," an anthology of plays it has produced. Out of the nine plays in the book, those written by Filipino American playwrights include Linda Faigao-Hall's "Woman From The Other Side of the World," Han Ong's "Middle Finger," Ong's co-written play "Savage Acts," Peña's "Flipzoids," and Peña's co-written play "Project: Balangiga." It also includes Lonnie Carter's "The Romance of Magno Rubio" and Chris Millado's "peregriNasyon."

In 2010, Ma-Yi received a Special Drama Desk Award for

Excellence for "more than two decades of excellence and for nurturing Asian American voices in stylistically varied and engaging theater."[49] The Drama Desk Awards were established in 1949 by a group of New York City theater critics, editors, reporters, and publishers.

*

In 2006, National Asian American Theatre Company (NAATCO) received the Rosetta LeNoire Award from Actors' Equity Association for significant contributions in increasing diversity and non-traditional casting. Founding artistic director Mia Katigbak received the 2014 Obie Award for Performance—for playing Bessie in NAATCO's staging of Clifford Odets' "Awake and Sing!"—and the 2016 Lilly Award in Trailblazing, which celebrates women of distinction in American theater.

*

In 2009, writer and editor Randy Gener (1967–) received the George Jean Nathan Award for Dramatic Criticism for his work in Theatre Communications Group's (TCG) American Theatre Magazine. The award's recipient is chosen by the heads of the English departments of Cornell, Princeton, and Yale Universities for "the American who has written the best piece of drama criticism during the theatrical year (July 1 to June 30), whether it is an article, an essay, treatise, or book."

The award committee's citation for Gener noted that he has focused on "largely ignored voices and visions on the international theatrical scene ... to the future of theatrical

---

[49] Ang. "Asian American playwrights lend support to their Filipino counterparts." *PDI*. Oct. 18, 2010.

criticism itself in essays that wed critical intelligence with a beat reporter's love of the telling and unruly fact."

Gener moved to the US from the Philippines in 1985. He studied journalism at University of Nevada-Reno and has been a writer and editor for various publications, including as arts critic for The Village Voice (1992–2001). He was connected with American Theatre Magazine from '02 to '12.

*

In 2011, the University of Kansas Endowment Association created the Paul Stephen Lim Asian American Playwriting Award to honor Lim's outstanding career as teacher, playwright, and advocate for new voices in American theater.

The award is given to student playwrights of Asian heritage and comes with membership to the Dramatists Guild (an organization for playwrights, composers, and lyricists established in 1921) and a development opportunity for the winning play at the John F. Kennedy Center for the Performing Arts' American College Theater Festival.

In a 2016 radio interview,[50] Lim mentioned that it has been "wonderful to see the kinds of plays that the younger Asian Americans are writing." He noted that the subject matter they tackle has shifted from "problems of integration or discrimination" to more mainstream topics, focusing "more on the similarities of the Asian American experience rather than the differences."

---

[50] Chen, Jen. "Full Circle: Acclaimed Playwright Paul Stephen Lim." KCUR 89.3 website: Kcur.org. Jun. 4, 2016. http://kcur.org/post/full-circle-acclaimed-playwright-paul-stephen-lim

San Dionisio sa America in Los Angeles

A community of Filipino immigrants from Manila has been keeping a religious devotional performance tradition alive in Los Angeles since the mid-1990s. San Dionisio sa America [San Dionisio in America] is collectively run by a group of families originally from the San Dionisio *barangay* [district] in Parañaque City, Metro Manila.

As the legend goes, after the first bishop of Paris, France was beheaded by pagans (circa the 250s AD), he picked up his head and walked for miles while preaching a sermon until he died. The bishop became regarded as Saint Denis, patron saint of the French people.

Devotees who live in the saint's namesake barangay in Parañaque City have a belief that San Dionisio would hurl his decapitated head if a *komedya* is not performed on his feast day. In other towns in the Philippines, komedya performances in honor of the saint are staged to ensure a good harvest.

Komedya is adapted from the Spanish theater form *comedia*, plays that feature royal characters from fictitious warring European and Middle Eastern kingdoms. Since komedya were used by Spanish colonizers as an evangelizing tool—where villainized Muslim stock characters are usually overcome or converted by heroic Christian stock characters—the genre is also commonly called *moro-moro*, derived from *moro*, the Spanish term for North African Muslims, i.e. moors. Classic komedya feature verse lines recited in a sing-song delivery; choreographed and stylized entrances, exits, and battles; and stories that usually have a romantic plot.

These days, participation in non-professional stagings of komedya, whether onstage or backstage, is borne out of devotion and tradition rather than prescribed by superstition. In the mid-1990s, the immigrants from San Dionisio started presenting komedya excerpts during their community gatherings. The snippets soon grew into full-length productions.

Joseph Herpacio, whose family has been involved with San Dionisio sa America (SDA) since its founding, moved to Los Angeles from the Philippines when he was 12 years old. "My family made me join every performance because they want the tradition to be passed on to the next generation," he said. Over the years, he has moved up from actor to fight choreographer to director. "It's also my *panata* [religious vow] to our patron saint. It's my way of giving back for all the blessings bestowed on me and my family."

Rick San Agustin had been involved with PETA in the early 1970s, moved to the US in 1977, and began his involvement with SDA in the mid-1990s. "I've been trying my best to bring SDA out to the mainstream Pilipino community of California," said San Agustin, whose father had been part of a komedya group that performed in San Dionisio and around Metro Manila.

"I believe that our komedya is a cultural gem that needs to be shared with the rest of our *kababayan* [countrymen] and the outside world." From initially just helping out with music scoring, he eventually shepherded the group from the small church halls they had been using to the much larger Barnsdall Theater in 2002, where they have since performed komedya every other year. Komedya they have performed include "Ang Kambal ng Valencia" ["The Twins of Valencia"] ('02); "Hermano de la Paz" ('04); "Nerissa at Bolivar" ["Nerissa and Bolivar"] ('06); "Esperanza at Caridad" ["Esperanza and Caridad"] ('08); and "Mga Prinsesa ng Cordova" ["The Princesses of Cordova"] ('10).

More Filipino American theater educators

Francis Tanglao-Aguas (1971–) moved to the US in 1987. He took up theater, then a master's in playwriting at University of California (UC)-Los Angeles, where he was also founding artistic director (1993–95) of Theater Underground, the university's resident undergraduate theater group. Since 2003, he has taught playwriting and theater-related subjects at Georgetown University in Washington, DC, Kenyon College in Ohio, and College of William and Mary in Virginia.

Plays he has written include "When the Purple Settles," "Abuja Woman," "Where the Carabao Sleeps," and "Ramayana La'ar." In 2007, he became the founding artistic director of theater group International Performance Arts eXchange, based in College of William and Mary. Filipino American playwrights that the group has staged include Michael Golamco ("Cowboy Versus Samurai").

Aside from directing and teaching, Aguas has also performed his solo show "The Sarimanok Travels," about the magical sarimanok bird being stolen from the land of Mahallikha, in several cities across the US.

Director and playwright Anton Juan (1950–) has taught at University of Notre Dame du Lac, Indiana since 2006, where he is artistic director of the school's New Playwright's Workshop. He previously taught theater at University of the Philippines and directed for Dulaang Unibersidad ng Pilipinas [University of the Philippines Theater] and Repertory Philippines, among other theater groups; though he still returns to Manila occasionally to direct productions there.

Juan took up higher studies in theater at Centre Universitaire International de Formation et des Recherches Dramatiques [International University Center for Training and Dramatic Research] in Nancy, France and has taken postdoctoral studies as a Fulbright Senior Fellow at the Library of Congress and at University of Hawaii. In 2011, he became founding artistic director of Moon Crane Theatre Company in Chicago.

Continuing against the odds
In 2004, Bindlestiff Studio lost its sidewalk-facing unit at the ground floor of the Plaza Hotel building. The structure was going to be demolished so that it could be replaced with a low-cost housing building.

In reaction to public outcry for the venue's preservation, the local government committed to building the shell of a 99-seat, black box theater for Bindlestiff in the basement of the housing complex that would be constructed. In exchange, Bindlestiff would have to raise funds to have the space outfitted.

In the following years, Bindlestiff held office space and performance venues in different sites while continuing with its programming and taking on the new, additional task of fundraising.

Gayle Romasanta served as artistic director for a few years starting in 2007. She had been part of Teatro ng Tanan and had been with Bindlestiff since 1998. "The idea of who our community was—it was changing," she said of the years when the group worked toward moving back into its original location.

"Before we moved out, we were not beholden to funders. We put on shows and made money from that to pay the rent and utilities. After we moved out, we grappled with having to answer to the city and those who were funding our programs. While we were serving the community, we were changing as an organization—from an independent space to one that had to be accountable and show how we were serving the community.

"We were growing and having growing pains. If it weren't for our volunteers and artists whom we depended on, it would have been so much harder to operate."

In 2011, Bindlestiff moved back to its original location but now in a new building, the Plaza Apartments. Alan Quismorio was appointed as artistic director that year, a position he held until '16. He joined Bindlestiff in '11 after being co-artistic director at Asian American Theater Company from '08 to '10, where he had started out as an actor in the mid-1990s.

"The challenges back then included a working board that had to learn how to support the new space both fiscally and administratively," he said. "Not to mention politically, as Bindlestiff Studio had an arrangement with the City of San Francisco that clearly defined City Hall's expectations of the space's use."

Part of the changes he introduced was to bring in artists and productions that did not have previous history with the group. "At the end of the day, when box-office profit and donor funding were lean and foundation support still considered us unproven, we were still able to find the camaraderie and family dynamics to keep the space afloat."

Coming together

In 2002, artists and scholars from theater and other performing arts disciplines gathered to prepare a study on the impact of their creative work on Filipino American communities. The project was organized by the National Federation of Filipino American Associations' Cultural Project Team: Reme Grefalda of QBd Ink, scholars Lucy Mae San Pablo Burns and Theodore Gonzalves (formerly the musical director of tongue in A mood), and Anna Alves, a former program associate of the Ford Foundation's Media, Arts and Culture Unit.

The project held a series of meetings that year in Washington, DC, Los Angeles, and San Diego with artists and community leaders to gather information and to discuss "cultural stewardship through artistic and cultural expression, education, and performing arts." Attendees to the first convening held in Washington, DC included theater makers Dom Magwili, Wilma Consul (formerly with Teatro ng Tanan), Allan Manalo of Bindlestiff, Andy Gaston of

Pintig Cultural Group, and Alleluia Panis of Kulintang Arts, among others.

With support from the Ford Foundation, their findings and recommendations were published the following year in "Towards A Cultural Community: Identity, Education and Stewardship in Filipino American Performing Arts." The publication provides a snapshot of the various outlets and groups that helped create, preserve, and disseminate culture, heritage, and history for Filipino American communities at the time.

Included is an essay on the historical context of Filipino American performing arts by Gonzalves and an analysis of Pilipino Cultural Nights by Burns. It also has a report by Grefalda that profiled the performing arts and cultural work done at the time in various Filipino American communities, as well as an analysis of the social units that contribute to the perpetuation of performance and cultural traditions such as social clubs, regional organizations, community centers, language schools, and religious devotional practices.

Gonzalves went on to edit the book "Stage Presence: Conversations with Filipino American Performing Artists" ('07), a collection of interviews with and personal essays by performing arts leaders and pioneers from dance, music, theater, etc.; and to write his book "The Day the Dancers Stayed" ('09), his in-depth study of Pilipino Cultural Nights. Burns went on to write her book "Puro Arte: Filipinos on the Stages of Empire" ('12), where she uses Filipino American theater as a way to study US-Philippine relations.

*

In 2003, during a retreat for Asian American, Latin American, and African American theater leaders organized by Theatre Communications Group, East West Players (EWP) artistic director Tim Dang proposed a bi-annual Asian American theater conference to be launched in conjunction with EWP's 40th Anniversary in '06.

Asian American theater companies Ma-Yi, NAATCO, EWP, Pan Asian Repertory Theatre (PAR), Mu Performing Arts (based in Minneapolis), and Second Generation (based in New York) went on to organize "Next Big Bang: The First Asian American Theater Conference" in Los Angeles in '06.

The Consortium of Asian American Theaters and Artists (CAATA) was born. Ma-Yi, NAATCO, and PAR then headed the first Asian American Theater Festival in New York the following year. Conferences and festivals have since been held in Minneapolis ('08), New York ('09), Los Angeles ('11), Philadelphia ('14), and Ashland, Oregon ('16), with the Philadelphia installment being the first to combine the conference and festival into a single event. CAATA board members include Jorge Ortoll, Mia Katigbak, Second Generation artistic director Victor Maog, and Mu Performing Arts artistic director Randy Reyes.

*

In 2009, Filipino American performers in New York also banded together. Billy Bustamante, Liz Casasola, and Brian Jose cofounded Broadway Barkada [Broadway Clique] when all three were acting in PAR's staging of "Imelda: A New Musical."

That year, two typhoons adversely affected several areas in the Philippines and the trio gathered the all-Filipino American cast to perform in a benefit concert "to raise funds to send back home. It was such a success that we kept producing events that mobilized the Pinoy artistic community," said Bustamante.

The group's mission has evolved to provide a community for Filipino artists to cultivate their talents, elevate their global impact, as well as educate audiences. "We now have a roster of over a hundred Pinoy artists and have performed all over the country, spreading the message of community and Pinoy pride," he added.

Bustamante (1981–) was born in Washington, DC, studied musical theater at University of the Arts in Philadelphia, and has performed on Broadway and at regional theaters. He became co-artistic director of B-Side Productions in New York in '16. Elizabeth "Liz" Casasola (1975–) was born and raised in Los Angeles; studied musical theater at American Musical and Dramatic Academy, New York; and was managing director of Diverse City Theater from '00 to '05. Brian Jose (1974–) was born in Indianapolis, Indiana; studied theater at Indiana University; and has performed on tour around the country, in Off-Broadway shows, and at various regional theater productions.

Nurturing new works

In 2004, Ma-Yi established its Ma-Yi Writers Lab to nurture and showcase Asian American playwrights. Founded by Korean American Sung Rno, Ma-Yi's playwright-in-residence at the time, the group allows members to receive feedback on drafts of their works from fellow playwrights. In many cases, work that begins in the Lab has gone on to production by Ma-Yi or with other theater organizations.

Rehana Lew Mirza (1978–) joined the Lab in 2005 and became its co-director from '11 to '14. Born in Bridgewater, New Jersey to a Filipino mother and a Pakistani father, Mirza studied dramatic writing at New York University (NYU)'s Tisch School of the Arts and took up a master's in playwriting at Columbia University. Mirza and her sibling Rohi cofounded Desipina & Co. in 2001 to produce works that promote "cross-pollinations of artistic, political, and cultural dialogues." The term "desipina" describes a woman of South Asian (desi) and Filipina (pina) heritage.

Desipina & Co.'s inaugural production in '02 was Mirza's play "Barriers," about a Chinese Pakistani family dealing with the loss, backlash, and prejudice against South Asians after the World Trade Center tragedy. It is considered the first play to address the incident from a Muslim perspective. Her "Soldier X" was staged by Ma-Yi in '15. The play is about an American soldier who returns from his deployment to Afghanistan and falls in love with his dead comrade's sibling while his therapist falls in love with him.

Clarence Coo (1977–) joined the Lab in 2012. Born in Manila, Coo moved to Alexandria, Virginia with his family when he was five years old. He studied literary and cultural studies at College of William and Mary, then took up a master's in playwriting at Columbia University. Coo was one of the four winners of the 1995 Young Playwrights Festival in New York City with his "Proof Through the Night," about an encounter between a suicidal diva and a homicidal janitor, which received a staging at The Public Theater.

He went on to write plays such as "Bahala Na (Let It Go)," about about an aging Chinese woman who conjures up memories of her life in China and the Philippines, in hopes of transforming her gay grandson, which was staged by Mu Performing Arts in '07; and "Beautiful Province," about a 15 year old boy who takes a road trip across Canada with his high school French teacher, which received the Yale Drama Series Award in '12, among others. His "People Sitting in Darkness," about a small town in the Philippines in 1901 preparing to stage a play based on an American novel about a young boy and an escaped slave rafting down the Mississippi river, has gone through a workshop production by Ma-Yi in '15.

A. Rey Pamatmat succeeded Mirza as the Lab's co-director in 2014. Pamatmat grew up in the Port Huron area in Michigan. He studied drama at NYU, took up a master's in playwriting at Yale University, and joined Ma-Yi's Writers Lab in '04. By the following year, his "Deviant" received a staging by Vortex Theatre Company. The play is about a lesbian couple's encounter with a male prostitute. His "Thunder Above, Deeps Below," about a "Filipina American, a Filipina transsexual, and a Puerto Rican hustler's struggle on Chicago's streets to scrounge up cash to bus it to San Francisco before the winter," was premiered by Second Generation in '09 and staged by Bindlestiff Studio in '12.

His "Edith Can Shoot Things and Hit Them," about two Filipino American siblings growing up in a remote Midwestern farm, partly inspired by the milieu of his own upbringing, was staged in succession in several theaters in different states as part of the National New Play Network's Rolling World Premiere program, which supports three or more theaters that mount the same new play within one year. In '15, it was staged in Boston simultaneously with his "after all the terrible things I do," about an immigrant Filipino American woman who hires a man who has a dark connection with her son. His first play to be staged by Ma-Yi was "House Rules" in '16, a comedy about two sets of Filipino American siblings coming to terms with their respective parents' mortality.[51]

*

When Teatro ng Tanan took up residence at Bindlestiff in 1998, its theater workshops were absorbed by the latter group. The workshops soon included classes in clown work, mask work, and commedia dell'arte. The component where directing students were paired with playwriting students for recitals was eventually called "Stories High."

Initially, a number in the title would denote the quantity of plays to be staged at the recitals, for example, "Six Stories High," "Eight and a Half Stories High," etc. Since then, "Stories High" has continued to be a regular component of Bindlestiff's programming.

Since 2006, Bindlestiff's "The Love Edition" (TLE) series has had an open call for plays that focus on stories about all manner of love and affection. Conceptualized by Bindlestiff actors and producers Chuck Lacson and Rafael "Raf" Lim as a follow-up endeavor to the "Stories High" program, TLE is meant to provide production opportunities for new works

---

[51] Ang. "Ma-Yi comedy on Fil-Am families opens in New York." *Inquirer.net.* Mar. 22, 2016. http://globalnation.inquirer.net/137978/137978

as well as existing material written by Bindlestiff members. The name of the series was borne out of being initially given a slot in February, thus the thematic link to Valentine's Day and love. The show proved popular with theatergoers and has been staged regularly since 2013. It has also grown to accept submissions nationwide.

Stories High and The Love Edition have not only inspired participants to pursue further work in theater and produced new collaborators for Bindlestiff, they have also helped train career playwrights such as Conrad Panganiban (1972–). Born in Monterey, California, Panganiban was inspired to become a playwright after hearing the audience's reaction to a script he wrote in 1995 for the PCN of California State University-Sacramento's Filipino Club.

"The approach was very *teleserye* [soap opera] with different character stories," he said. "There were serious and comedic moments throughout the play, but when I first heard the audience laugh at something I wrote, I was hooked!" Panganiban was a business major at the time. "For many Filipino Americans in college campuses, a PCN is the closest we come to being in theater," he added.

He soon discovered and joined Sinag-tala Filipino Theater and Performing Arts Association ["Sinag-tala" is Tagalog for "Starlight"], a community group in Sacramento, California founded by Alcide "Sonny" Alforque in 1990 that provides free theater workshops.[52] "From there, I found out about

---

[52] Alforque, Angela-Dee. "Transnational Stages: Prospectus for a Filipino American Theater." *Philippine Sociological Review*, Vol. 48, 2000. Quezon City: Philippine Sociological Society.

Bindlestiff Studio and their Stories High workshops."

Panganiban wrote his first short plays with Bindlestiff and seeing them produced on stage fueled what had become a hobby into being seriously considered as a career. He went on to complete a master's in creative writing with a focus on playwriting at SF State.

"I can honestly say that without Sinag-tala and Bindlestiff, I wouldn't be where I'm at today with wanting to write about events from Filipino American history and topics that affect the Filipino American." His one-act "Esperanza Means Hope," about domestic violence, received stagings in 2012; and his one-act "Inay's Wedding Dress," about two Filipino American sisters and their mother's bequeathed wedding dress, was staged by Bindlestiff in 2014.[53] ["Inay" is "mom."]

*

In 2013, Thelma Virata de Castro (1966–) founded San Diego Playwrights, a network of playwrights who work on joint projects to encourage production opportunities for local writers in San Diego.

"Playwrights have the unique position of existing at the intersection of the literary and performing arts," she wrote in a blog post detailing the genesis of the group. "I can't just write a play and be done with it. It needs to be performed. San Diego playwrights need to be produced in order to grow. We want to be involved in local theater as more than audience members.

---

[53] Ang. "Play inspired by labor leader Larry Itliong to premiere in SF."

"Playwrights can't exist in isolation ... we have to get out there and be seen and be heard. San Diego playwrights need to take responsibility for our own careers and build a community that supports us. In this reciprocal relationship, we must determine what the community wants and needs from us. We must give back so that all our interests are met."

To this end, she surveyed local playwrights to determine their needs and resources. "I put out a monthly email with opportunities and news. We've partnered with theaters and other organizations for events and workshops. We have a monthly feedback evening called WordPlay Tuesdays with Diversionary Theatre."

Born in San Diego, De Castro studied English literature at UCLA and has taken playwriting workshops with different organizations such as EWP's David Henry Hwang Writer's Institute. She was literary manager at San Diego Asian American Repertory Theatre from '02 to '05.

De Castro has been writing plays actively since the 1990s. Two of her one-acts received staged readings at EWP in 1993. Her work has been staged by Fritz Theatre and Carlsbad Playhouse, among others. Some of her plays with Filipino American characters or themes include "The Goddess of Flowers," where Filipino American Flora is haunted by the myth of a mysterious flying man, staged by San Diego Asian American Repertory Theatre in '02; and one-act "Meet the Family," where accusations of crimes greet a young Filipino American woman when she brings home a man to meet her family, staged in the Fritz Blitz of New Plays by California Writers in San Diego in '06.

Excerpts of "Meet the Family" where also performed that same year by CIRCA-Pintig.

Staging more stories
Nibras Arab American Theater

In 2001, Maha Chehlaoui, whose mother is Filipino and father is Syrian, founded Nibras Arab American Theater in New York City. ["Nibras" is Arabic for "lamp" or "lantern leading the way."] The group's aim is to increase positive visibility and creative expression of Arabs and Arab Americans. She served as Nibras' founding artistic director until '05. Chehlaoui's founding of the group was partly inspired by the work of Ma-Yi Theater in its staging of Filipino works in its early years.

She found out about Ma-Yi from one of her mother's friends. "That one of my parents' friends knew of a small Off-Broadway theater group and that she spoke of it with such pride—it left an impression on me. I was used to my parents' generation being mainly interested in Broadway," she said. "It resonated with me that people like to see their own stories on stage. The importance of representation has become a centerpiece of my own personal mission. In the aftermath of 9/11, I saw my Arab community being vilified, spoken for as though none of us could speak.

"It felt urgent to create space for our voices. A matter of survival. It is important not just for those of us who tend to be invisible or stereotyped in mainstream culture, but for society as a whole. When we split off entire communities from our consciousness it allows us to do incredible harm. How often have we looked back and said 'I can't believe we used to think it was ok to do that?' This work empowers those rarely heard, and also, when done well, helps close that empathy gap that so many marginalized bodies are falling into."

Born in New Jersey, Chehlaoui studied for a master's in acting at Columbia University and has acted in, directed, and produced works with theater companies in New York and in other states. She was the executive director of Noor Theatre in New York City from '08 to '16, where she handled strategic planning and programming development. ["Noor" is Arabic for "light" or "bright."] The group is dedicated to supporting and presenting the work of theater artists of Middle Eastern heritage.

Diverse City Theater

In 2003, actor, director, and dancer Victor Lirio founded Diverse City Theater Company (DCT) in New York City to promote new plays and emerging playwrights "that portray our society's evolving cultural and lifestyle diversity issues as well as promote non-traditional casting of actors." Lirio moved to San Francisco from Manila when he was 11 years old and later trained as a dancer at the Academy of Ballet. He later relocated to New York to further his dance training.

"I was very successful in getting callbacks at dance calls, often making it to the final callbacks, but I was also often typed out due to my God-given size—short and slightly built," he said. "I was on the road for the first national tour of the 1996 Broadway revival of 'The King and I' when I started reflecting on my artistic goals and career trajectory. I had felt unfulfilled as a chorus dancer," he said, which led to his further training in acting.

"When I started DCT, I was desperate for work like most Asian actors. I had become part of Ensemble Studio Theatre's community, under the mentorship of its founder, the late Curt Dempster. I was introduced to a spirited and passionate community of theater makers: playwrights, directors, and actors." Lirio collaborated with the group during summer residencies, which then birthed DCT's play incubator program Green Room Series.

"I curated and produced the program, working closely with the playwrights and our resident dramaturg Maxine Kern. It was during this practical process that I was able to hone my directing skills. I started directing readings first, and my work evolved into full productions."

DCT's inaugural production was Linda Faigao-Hall's "The Female Heart," about Anghel (played by Lirio), who has a life-threatening disease, and his sibling, Adelfa, who becomes a mail-order bride to a man from Brooklyn in order to pay for Anghel's medical bills.

DCT's Green Room Series went on to develop over 35 original plays under different themes: third-world poverty ('05), gender identity ('06), women and their generation ('07), re-examination of the American identity in the 21st century ('08), race and social politics ('09).

In 2010, DCT produced "The Pearl Project," a Filipino American theater festival that featured Eric Gamalinda's "Resurrection," about the unexplained suicide of a young woman and its effects on her family; and Jorshinelle Taleon-Sonza's "The Encounter," about the unexpected visit of an incumbent Philippine president to his political rival's prison cell. It also featured two one-acts by Kristine Reyes: "Quarter Century Baby," where the surprise visit of two parents to their Filipino daughter and her American boyfriend reveals painful truths, and "Something Blue," about an estranged father's quest to reconnect with his daughter on her wedding day. DCT was active until late 2011, when Lirio relocated to another state.

Mezclao Productions

Actor, dancer, playwright, choreographer, and director Giovanni Ortega (1976–) founded Mezclao Productions in Los Angeles in 2003. "We provide an outlet for artists to garner social and cultural awareness in promotion of tolerance and acceptance," he said.

The group has staged works such as "Lazy Juan and the Bee Powder," an adaptation of a Filipino folktale; "Kalayaan," about Muslim identity ["Kalayaan" is "freedom"]; and "Kwentong Pinoy," about Filipino and Filipino American identity and displacement ["Kwentong Pinoy" translates to "Pinoy Stories"]. From '09 to '13, through Mezclao, he was producing artistic director for civic group Search to Involve Pilipino Americans' Performance Space.

Born in Metro Manila, Ortega moved to the US in 1989. "I've always been interested in performance and writing. I was hooked when I did my first musical 'The Wiz,' in eighth grade." He has a master's in performance from UCLA and has been involved with productions either as an actor or director at EWP, Kulintang Arts, and other groups. He also teaches at Pomona College's Department of Theatre and Dance.

Aside from his play "Allos, the story of Carlos Bulosan" ('11), commissioned by EWP for its Theater for Youth Program, he has also written "Criers for Hire," about Filipino American women hired to cry at funerals, commissioned by EWP for its 50th anniversary season in '16.[54]

Berserker Residents

In 2007, actor and dancer Justin Jain cofounded alternative comedy group Berserker Residents with David Johnson and Bradley Wrenn in Philadelphia. The group stages shows that combine physical theater, puppetry, music, sketch, and prop comedy. It has created shows "Jersey Devil" ('07), "The Giant Squid" ('08), and "Annihilation Point" ('11). A native of Florida, Jain studied acting at University of the Arts in Philadelphia. He performs with various companies regionally and teaches theater-related subjects at University of the Arts.

Chalk Repertory Theatre

In 2008, actor and director Jennifer Chang cofounded Chalk Repertory Theatre in Los Angeles and served as its artistic producing director until '16. The group is dedicated to producing classical and contemporary plays in unconventional spaces. Born in San Francisco, Chang studied acting at NYU's Tisch School of the Arts and took up a master's in acting at UC San Diego. In 2016, she became head of the undergraduate acting program at UC San Diego. She has been involved in acting, directing or play development with groups such as Playwrights' Arena, EWP, and NAATCO, among others.

---

[54] Ang. "Fil-Am play 'Criers for Hire' on Los Angeles stage in February." *Inquirer.net.* Jan. 28, 2016. http://globalnation.inquirer.net/135751/135751

Creative Destruction

Nelson Eusebio III (1977–) cofounded theater collective Creative Destruction in 2008 in New York City and served as its artistic director until 2011. "Growing up in New Jersey, theater was really for white people," said Eusebio, who was born in Philadelphia. "When we moved to San Diego, theater there was much more diverse. There, I experienced that it was for everybody—Latin American, African American, Asian American, you name it. This idea changed my whole life. I felt empowered to really try new things."

He did theater throughout high school and later joined the Marines partly to earn funding for college. Eusebio studied drama at UC Irvine and for a master's in directing at Yale University's School of Drama. He has developed and directed work for Ma-Yi, PAR, South Coast Repertory, Laguna Playhouse, and Mark Taper Forum, among others.

Leviathan Lab

In 2009, actor and director Ariel Estrada (1969–) founded Leviathan Lab in New York City to provide a space where Asian American artists can find a home, grow, and experiment. "One of the many glaring inequities between Asian American theater artists and our white counterparts is the sheer amount of chances they get to develop their craft in professional settings in the early parts of their careers," he said.

"There were precious few chances in New York City for Asian and Pacific Islander (API) actors to do that when I first came to this city in 1997. Even less now, as the major API-centered theaters have moved to Off-Broadway contracts, which leaves early-career API theater artists at an extreme disadvantage. Leviathan seeks to remedy that."

Estrada, who was born in Jersey City, New Jersey, has been doing theater and music since middle school. "An incredible public school teacher, Ginny Packer, who truly loved teaching arts to young people, cast me in the school musical. I've been hooked ever since."

Leviathan Lab had Nelson Eusebio as artistic director from '10 to '12, Estrada from '13 to '14, and Flordelino Lagundino since '14. Estrada continues to serve as a board member of the group.

Current Theatrics
Playwright and director Ruth Pe Palileo (1971–) cofounded Current Theatrics in 2010. Born in Antique province, Palileo moved to Detroit with her family in 1974. "The first play I directed was at Holy Redeemer Catholic School. It was 'Hansel and Gretel' and I was five years old," she said.

In 2006, she met Angela Mascarenas, who asked her to write a play for CIRCA-Pintig. "I wrote a playlet called 'High Stakes' ('07), where women playing mahjong also competed with each other in how many third world babies they can adopt." Palileo has since been involved with the group, where she focuses on drama for children with autism.

Current Theatrics, which she cofounded with Irish American Thomas Costello, is based in Las Vegas. The pair met in Ireland when Palileo was studying for a doctorate in theatre and performance at Trinity College in Dublin.

"We focus on creating traveling theater. We find an event

or place that wants a specific story to be told, for example, a London science-fiction convention wanted a time-travel play. Then we craft the show so it can be traveled to that location."

Palileo's ethos for the group was partly inspired by the props used in Honolulu theater company Kumu Kahua's 1998 production of "peregriNasyon" that toured Manila—pieces of custom-built luggage that fit into each other and contained the cast's costumes and other props.

"My imagination was fired by the idea of packing up a show into suitcases, traveling with everybody as a team and then arriving, as theater sojourners, just long enough to create the gift of art."

Palileo has been a member of the Association for Theatre in Higher Education since '14. In 2015, she became involved with the Senior Theatre Group, a group of scholars who focus on theater for seniors.

Artigiani Troupe

In 2012, actor and director Orlando Pabotoy founded Artigiani Troupe in New York City, a theater group composed of clowns and commedia dell'arte artisans, and serves as its artistic director. Pabotoy, whose father is Filipino, was born and raised in Delapaz, Bohol province.

His family moved to the US in 1991. He shifted from physics at George Mason University, Virginia to acting at The Juilliard School (Juilliard), New York. He cofounded the Clown School in Los Angeles in 2007 with David Bridel and was responsible for creating the curriculum. He was involved with the school until 2010.

"The main thing for me is that commedia dell'arte and clown work champions the childlike approach to working in theater," he said. "It keeps the possibility of 'playfulness' alive in the approach of any process and in any project. Playfulness as practice transcends style and artistic borders."

He has worked with groups such as Ma-Yi, The Public Theater, La MaMa, Old Globe Theatre, Yale Repertory Theater, and Center Theatre Group, among others. He is a faculty member at NYU's Tisch School of the Arts.

People Of Interest

Director and choreographer Jesca Prudencio (1986–) founded People Of Interest in 2014. "My passion lies in working on community-specific issues and experimenting with different theatrical forms," she said. The group stages works in the US and internationally, with its inaugural production, "FAN: stories from the brothels of Bangkok," staged in Thailand. The New Jersey-native studied drama at NYU and took up a master's in directing at UC San Diego.

She was previously the education director ('08-'13) and is currently the lead trainer for Ping Chong and Company. Prudencio has also developed work with companies like EWP, La MaMa, The Old Vic, and others.

More playwrights

Though Michael Golamco's (1975–) first play "Achievers" premiered in 2001, what helped gained him notice was his

"Cowboy Versus Samurai." In the play, a Korean American man falls in love with an Asian American woman who only dates white men. Premiered in '05 by NAATCO, it has since been staged across the US. Golamco moved to the San Francisco Bay Area from Manila in 1985 and went on to study English literature at UCLA.

Though initially wanting to be a novelist, he began to write plays after cofounding Lapu, the Coyote that Cares (LCC) Theatre Company, an Asian American theater group at UCLA, in 1995. He has also written "Year Zero" ('09), about a Cambodian American man who deals with loneliness by talking to a human skull in a cookie jar, and "Build" ('12), about two video game designers' encounters with technology and artificial intelligence, among others.

*

Jorshinelle Taleon-Sonza (1946–) moved to the US in 1984. "I became a playwright by chance," she said. "After completing my doctorate in comparative literature at Drew University, New Jersey, I wanted a break from academia. I had always enjoyed the theater and, hoping to do something 'fun,' I enrolled in a playwriting program at the The New School in New York. I enjoyed it so much, I decided to become a playwright."

In 2002, her "Sandman," about a daughter's discovery of her mother's past actions against an abuser, and "Migration Blues," a trilogy of one-acts about the personal struggles and cultural conflicts of Filipino Americans, received a staging.

"How to Cook Adobo," one of the one-acts from the trilogy, about three generations of women whose arguments on how best to cook chicken adobo serve as a metaphor for assimilation into American culture, received a staged reading by DCT, which led to Victor Lirio commissioning other works from her.

Her other plays include "Cold Flesh" ('06), about a Filipino American man who has a wife in the Philippines but has an affair with a man; and "Lena's Way" ('12), about a woman's jealous reaction to her communist ex-boyfriend's new love.

"I write about the Filipino experience in America, particularly about the lives of domestic helpers, suburban housewives, and hospital workers who confront issues such as homelessness, racial discrimination, and exile," she said. Taleon-Sonza has published anthologies of her work, including "Dog Days in America and Other Plays" ('12) and "Haiyan and Other Plays about the Homeland" ('16).

*

In 2005, Kristine Reyes (1979–) worked under DCT's First Draft Fellowship—with Linda Faigao-Hall as a mentor—to develop "Queen for a Day," a play where family tensions erupt when teenager Nicole and her mother go to Ohio to take care of her aunt.

Reyes moved to the US from the Philippines with her family when she was four years old. After studying English at Goucher College, Maryland, she moved to New York City to pursue playwriting. "Linda was the first Asian and Filipino American writer and teacher that I had ever had. She was a wonderful mentor to me when I was just learning the ropes of playwriting. She taught me a lot of fundamentals," Reyes said.

"She also provided a lot of inspiration to me, to see another Filipino American woman writer who was a veteran in the industry. It meant that there was already a path paved for me. I'm really grateful to have had that experience with Linda so early on in my career."

She eventually became a playwright associate at DCT and a writer-in-residence at Mission to (dit)Mars, a theater organization that supports new plays by theater artists in Queens, New York. Her works have been performed across the country.

Her one-act "Lola Luning's First Steps," about how Luning, her daughter, and granddaughter grapple with the aftermath of sexual and domestic violence ["Lola" is "grandmother"], was commissioned and produced by Women of Color Productions. Her short comedy "Balikbayan Birthday," about two siblings in the Philippines and their excitement over their mother's return from years of working abroad ["Balikbayan" is "repatriate"], was developed with Leviathan Lab.

*

Born and raised in Palo Alto, California, Boni Alvarez worked as an actor first before shifting to playwriting. He studied theater at Sarah Lawrence College, acted in New York, and took up a master's in acting at Harvard University. "After grad school, I went back to New York. I had an agent, I was part of Actors' Equity, but I wasn't getting very many auditions," he said.

Alvarez had taken several playwriting classes in college and remembered a professor telling him that he had potential as a playwright. "I took some more playwriting classes and, after a few years, went to the University of Southern California for a master's in dramatic writing."[55]

Jon Lawrence Rivera had attended a reading of Alvarez's thesis "Ruby, Tragically Rotund" and committed to producing the play about Filipino American college student Ruby, whose tuition money has been used by her mother to fund Ruby's sibling's pursuit of a beauty pageant title. Alvarez graduated in '07 and Playwrights' Arena staged the play in '09 to sold-out houses and an extended run.

"Ruby" featured Los Angeles-based one-person show performer Alison De La Cruz in the title role. De La Cruz began performing as a poet and spoken-word artist in 1998, having trained at EWP's David Henry Hwang Writer's Institute and under other playwrights. She has developed works that touch on identity, gender, sexuality, and memory such as "Sungka" and "Naturally Graceful." [Sungka is a Filipino mancala game.]

Now based in Los Angeles, Alvarez's other produced works with Filipino American themes include "Dallas Non-Stop" ('13), where a call-center agent in the Philippines tries to acquire a US visa; and "Bloodletting" ('16), where two Filipino American siblings encounter a Filipino supernatural creature. His works have been developed or staged in New York, Phoenix, Philadelphia, and at the Oregon Shakespeare Festival.

---

[55] Ang. "Fil-Am playwright Boni Alvarez brings aswang to Los Angeles." *Inquirer.net*. Mar. 30, 2017. http://usa.inquirer.net/2491/fil-playwright-boni-alvarez-brings-aswang-los-angeles

Directing and leading

In 2003, Michelle Aguillon (1966–) became president of Hovey Players in Waltham, Massachusetts. She served this position until '08. She has been involved with the group since 1995 and has been a trustee since '13. Born north of the San Francisco Bay Area, Aguillon studied acting at the Royal National Theatre in London.

"I played Santa's elf in my sixth grade Christmas play where I had one line, which produced a laugh, and I was hooked," she said. She has directed productions for Metro Stage Company and Turtle Lane Playhouse, among others. She cofounded and was director of theater group Sox of Red Productions in Los Angeles from '08 to '09.

*

In 2007, Flordelino Lagundino (1970–) founded Thunder Mountain Theatre Project in Juneau, Alaska (renamed Generator Theater Company in '09), where he served as artistic director until '16. He previously cofounded Tsunami Theatre with Indonesian American Joan Rebecca Taylor in 1997 in Washington, DC (where he was born and raised), where he was artistic director until 1999.

After finishing his master's in acting at Brown University, Rhode Island, Lagundino first visited Juneau in 2005 to work as an actor in Perseverance Theatre's staging of "The Long Season," a musical written by Chay Yew with music by Fabian Obispo, about Filipino Alaskan cannery worker Allos fighting to gain the respect of the foreman, the faith of the other workers, and the heart of the foreman's spouse.

Along with playwright Merry Ellefson and director Paul

Joseph Paparelli, Lagundino conducted interviews with 20 Filipino Americans in Juneau and Anchorage over eight months—which included Ellery Lumbab, founding artistic director of Alitaptap Filipino Dance Troupe [Firefly Filipino Dance Troupe]. The interviews were then used to create "Voyage," written by Ellefson, about four generations of Filipino Alaskans. The production was co-directed by Paparelli and Lagundino.[56]

Lagundino continued to work with both Generator Theater and Perseverance Theatre, acting in or directing productions. Lagundino has acted in and directed productions with companies across the US. In '14, he was appointed artistic director of Leviathan Lab in New York.

*

In 2012, Victor Malana Maog (1972–) was appointed the artistic director of Second Generation theater company in New York City. Born in Metro Manila, Maog moved to Hayward, California in 1979. "I discovered forensics, competitive speech and debate, and drama at James Logan High School," he said.

His first professional directing work was for Teatro ng Tanan (TnT) in 1993. He had read about their work while he was a struggling actor in New York and he reached out to them. "They were very welcoming and encouraged me to connect when I returned to the Bay Area." Maog was given the opportunity to direct TnT's production of Edgar Poma's "Little Train." Though it was his only project with the group, "It kickstarted my directing career—a career that has

---

[56] "'Voyage' gives voice to Filipino history." *CapitalCityWeekly.com*. Apr. 20, 2005. http://capitalcityweekly.com/stories/042005/news_20050420040.shtml

brought me to so many different stages nationally and internationally," he said.

After his stint with TnT, he was appointed artistic director of San Joaquin County's Theatre Arts Project. The program paid economically disadvantaged youth to perform full-scale, free-of-charge outdoor musicals to audiences of 500 to 4,000. During his tenure, Maog was able to cast Filipino immigrants who had formerly worked in farms in the program's shows. "With a diverse cast, the classic musicals like 'Damn Yankees' and 'The Music Man,' were making these former asparagus fields farmers sing with a new and revolutionary '76 Trombones!'"

He went on to take up performance studies at NYU and continues to work as a director and educator in professional, educational, and community-based settings. "Where I can, I try to open the doors for diverse staff hires and unique casting choices. My Cyrano was an African American. Prospero was Filipino. Malvolio was Trinidadian. I have had the good fortune to direct works by Latino, Caucasian, Middle Eastern, Native American, and African American writers."

*

In 2013, Randy Reyes (1972–) was appointed artistic director of Mu Performing Arts in Minneapolis, Minnesota. Born in Metro Manila, Reyes and his family moved to California when he was a child. He went on to study acting at University of Utah on a scholarship, then at Juilliard. Frustrated at the lack of opportunities for Asian American actors in New York, he started acting for regional theaters. After a stint with the Guthrie Theater, where he did acting and education work, he relocated to Minneapolis in the mid-2000s.

In 2006, he received TCG's New Generations Future Leaders Mentorship grant to work under Mu's founding artistic director Rick Shiomi. "It was an amazing two-year grant that allowed me to learn the inner workings of being the artistic director with Rick," said Reyes.

Shiomi assigned Reyes to direct Filipino American Marcus Quiniones' (a native of Molokai, Hawaii) "Circle Around the Island," an autobiographical movement-based play that Quiniones had directed, choreographed, and performed for Mu earlier in 1999. This opened a path for Reyes to continue in directing other works.

As Mu's artistic director, Reyes oversees season lineup selection, budgeting and fundraising, marketing and administration, hiring and human resources, curriculum development, and outreach programming.[57]

*

Born and raised in Covington, Virginia, May Adrales' work as a freelance director spans across the country. After studying literature and theater at University of Virginia, she moved to New York and explored playwriting, dramaturgy, and directing. Realizing that directing was the path she was meant for, she studied for a master's degree in it at Yale University's School of Drama and has since built a positive reputation for working on premieres of new material.

---

[57] Ang. "Fil-Am director-actor named to board of nat'l theater group." *Inquirer.net*. Aug. 24, 2017. http://usa.inquirer.net/6140/fil-director-actor-named-board-natl-theater-group

She has been an artistic associate and faculty member at The Public Theater, spearheading its Shakespeare Lab ('06–'09); On Site Programs Director at Lark Play Development Center ('08–'10); and has directed and taught at Juilliard, NYU, Brown University, and Yale University. Adrales has been appointed as Milwaukee Repertory Theater's Associate Artistic Director for its 2017–18 season.

Philippines onstage

Events in or issues related to the Philippines continue to be a source of subject matter for Filipino American theater works.

Ma-Yi revived its "Flipzoids" in 2011. "We've had many requests to bring back the play," explained playwright and director Ralph Peña of the company's decision to remount his play. "We haven't done a Filipino [themed] play since 'The Romance of Magno Rubio' in 2003. We've noticed a drop in attendance from Filipino audiences and this restaging is our courtship song to get them back. Heck, there's a new generation of Filipino Americans who haven't seen the play and we're hopeful they will find it meaningful."

"Finally, the national discourse on identity has deepened since 'Flipzoids' was last staged [in 1996]. Don't get me wrong, racial bigotry is very much alive and well in America, and our colonial baggage continues to weigh down Filipinos in this country, but I think the play itself needs to make a tonal shift to reflect how today's immigrants see themselves. Simply declaring 'I want or don't want to belong' seems overly simplistic to me now.

There are so many more intermediary shadings between these polar positions that I find much more interesting."[58]

*

The musical "Prison Dancer," about Filipino inmates who become famous after videos of their dancing become an online sensation, debuted at the New York Musical Theatre Festival in 2012. The production was inspired by a video that went viral on the internet in '07. It featured inmates of the Cebu Provincial Detention and Rehabilitation Center in the Philippines dancing en masse to Michael Jackson's "Thriller." The maximum-security prison had been having its prisoners perform synchronized movement routines as part of their daily exercise, then posting the videos of the routines online.

Created by Filipino Canadian theater makers, with music and lyrics by Romeo Candido and book by Carmen de Jesus, the musical was workshopped twice in '10 in Toronto prior to its US staging.

For the show's US premiere, Jose Llana was cast as one of the male leads while Filipino Canadian Jeigh Madjus reprised his role as Ruperto "Lola" Poblador. The cast received the Best Ensemble Award and Madjus received the Best Actor Award at the festival.

*

In 2016, Bindlestiff Studio staged "Tagalog: A Festival of One-Acts," three plays performed in Tagalog with English supertitles. The run sold out and proved popular enough that the company has already planned on doing another

---

[58] Ang. "Celebrated Fil-Am play to be restaged in New York." *PDI*. Jan. 17, 2011.

installment in '17. The three plays were selected from the Virgin Labfest, an annual showcase of new one-act plays that has been held in Manila since '04. Bindlestiff's artistic director at the time, Lorna Velasco, said that "there is a hunger from the audience to hear Tagalog spoken on stage."

When she directed "A Pinoy Midsummer" ('12), an adaptation of William Shakespeare's "A Midsummer Night's Dream," where some characters spoke in Tagalog, she "felt how the energy of the audience shifted, as if they sat up taller and leaned forward just to hear every single Tagalog word uttered." This observation inspired her to consider staging a production exclusively in Tagalog. "It's a dream for a lot of Filipino Americans here in the States to have more exposure to our languages, whether it's Tagalog, Ilocano, Kapampangan, or Visayan. We miss it, we miss home."[59]

Silver anniversaries

In the mid-2010s, several theater companies that were founded by Filipino American theater artists celebrated their 25th anniversaries.

Ma-Yi Theater Company's silver anniversary brochure states, "Two and a half decades is a long time, but we've always known we were in for a long, bumpy ride. That's what it takes to make change happen. When we started Ma-Yi Theater Company in 1989, we struggled to find Asian American plays to produce, and Asian American actors to

---

[59] Ang. "In San Francisco-'Tagalog,' three short plays about love." *Inquirer.net.* Apr. 5, 2016. http://globalnation.inquirer.net/138357/in-san-francisco-tagalog-three-short-plays-about-love

put on stage. That is no longer the case. Twenty-five years later, we have the Ma-Yi Writers Lab, the largest ever assembly of professional Asian American playwrights. Plays hatched at the Lab have made their way to prestigious regional houses around the country ... Today we have a national footprint, name recognition and credibility around the world. Today, Ma-Yi Theater is recognized as the country's leader in developing new works by Asian American playwrights. Our work is guided by knowing why and for whom we make theater."

National Asian American Theater Company founding artistic director Mia Katigbak said, "It's a milestone, just for the sheer fact that we have survived that long. I believe we enjoy the fortunate reputation of doing good work, no matter what we do, and that's a good thing. The anniversary affords me the opportunity to assess what NAATCO has accomplished thus far, and it is a good place from which to look to the future. To concoct other strategies for Asian American representation, visibility, and dynamism on the American stage. To reach other constituencies beyond the usual and to forge more meaningful partnerships with other non-Asian American theater artists and organ-izations."[60]

Playwrights' Arena founding artistic director Jon Lawrence Rivera said, "I'm a bit overwhelmed that we've lasted this long. It's a proud moment for me and for the company to have launched many careers. Especially since most of them are writers of color." He still sees "an overwhelming number of productions that have an all-white cast because

---

[60] Ang. "Obie-winning Mia Katigbak pushes for more Asian faces on the American stage."

the theater's white artistic director or the play's white director goes to their 'default' choice, which is white." Rivera is frustrated by productions set in major cities like Los Angeles, San Francisco, San Diego, Chicago, or New York but have no actor of color. "How is that possible? We still have a long way to go, in terms of diversity," he said. Nonetheless, he's seen some improvement. "I find that if the theater artistic head or a production's director is a person of color, then we see an increase of diverse artists involved in the process. It's also great how much our talent pool keep rising up to the challenges. The quality of acting has improved greatly and some are moving up in ranks and going to big regional theaters and on to Broadway."[61]

CIRCA-Pintig's Angela Mascarenas highlighted the pride in being able to continuously contribute to transformative social change. "The group's ability to continue to bring insightful, thought-provoking, collectively-produced original works for over two decades is already a huge accomplishment in itself," she said. "It says a lot about the people who volunteer and commit to this type of community work. It also says a lot about the communities that we get our support from. It truly has taken a village to make CIRCA-Pintig alive this long."[62]

Continuing engagement

The 2010s also saw several major productions on Off-Broadway and on Broadway with Filipino Americans in lead or feature roles or backstage involvement.

---

[61] Ang. "LA director soldiers on to boost new voices."
[62] Ang. "Chicago's Circa Pintig theater group gets set for 25th year."

In 2011, composer Robert Lopez, whose father is Filipino,[63] received Tony Awards for Best Book and Best Score (along with Trey Parker and Matt Stone for both awards) for "Book of Mormon." He previously received a Tony for Best Score for "Avenue Q" in '04.

In 2013, the Off-Broadway production of "Here Lies Love" opened with a predominantly Filipino American cast. The show returned in '14 for another run. Also in 2013, investing producer Jhett Tolentino became involved with a Tony-winning show, "Vanya and Sonia and Masha and Spike," which received Best Play. Tolentino had partnered with Joan Raffe to combine his passion for theater and her finances into a company that invested in Broadway productions.[64] Other productions they have invested in that have received Tony Awards include "A Raisin in the Sun" for Best Revival of a Play and "A Gentleman's Guide to Love and Murder" for Best Musical, both in '14.

In 2014, Celina "Lena Hall" Carvajal, whose father is of Filipino heritage, received the Tony Award for Best Featured Actress in a Musical for playing Yitzhak in the revival of "Hedwig and the Angry Inch." The San Francisco-native debuted on Broadway in '99 in "Cats" as Demeter and originated the role of Nicola in the musical "Kinky Boots" in '13. Darren Criss, also a San Francisco-native whose mother is Filipino, was cast as Hedwig in '15. He debuted on Broadway in '12 as J. Pierrepont Finch in the revival of "How to Succeed in Business Without Really Trying."

---

[63] Nepales. "Fil-Am composer wins Oscars' best song for Frozen's 'Let It Go.'" *PDI*. Mar. 3, 2014.
[64] Ang. "Pinoy Broadway producer gets Tony nominations—again." *PDI*. May 16, 2015.

Also in 2014, Chester See, who was born in Fairfield, California and whose mother is Filipino, was cast as Stacee Jaxx in the musical "Rock of Ages." That year, "Disney's Aladdin" opened on Broadway with Adam Jacobs as Aladdin and Don Darryl Rivera as antagonist henchman Iago. Jacobs, whose mother is Filipino, was born in Half Moon Bay, California and made his Broadway debut as Marius in "Les Miserables" in '07. Seattle-native Rivera's father Danny was a founding member of Filipino folk dance group Kultura.

Both Jacobs and Rivera originated their respective roles in the musical's world premiere in Seattle ('11) and went on to develop the characters further in the Toronto run ('13–'14) prior to opening the show's Broadway run. Jacobs will reprise the Aladdin role for the show's national tour which will begin in 2017, along with Reggie de Leon who has been cast as Iago. (Jacobs' sibling Arielle played Princess Jasmine in the Australia production in '16; she previously played Nina in the Broadway run and first national tour of "In The Heights," and Nessarose in the Broadway run of "Wicked.")

Two actors from "Here Lies Love," Jose Llana and Conrad Ricamora, went on to play the King of Siam and Lun Tha, respectively, in the 2015–16 Broadway revival of "The King and I" at the Lincoln Center. In the same show, Jon Viktor Corpuz played Chulalongkorn. A native of Florida, Corpuz was still studying at the Professional Performing Arts School when he was cast.[65] He was previously cast in a one-night-only presentation of "Godspell on Broadway Cast of 2032," where young actors performed roles from the

---

[65] Ang. "Fil-Am Jon Viktor Corpuz dazzles as Chulalongkorn in 'The King and I' Broadway revival." *PDI*. Jun. 27, 2015.

musical "Godspell." Also in 2015, Gabrielle "Gabby" Gutierrez, who had previously played Annie Who in the national tour of "How the Grinch Stole Christmas" ('14), was cast as one of the Matildas for the national tour of the musical "Matilda."

Also in 2015, Lea Salonga was cast as Kei Kimura in the Broadway production of "Allegiance,"[66] a musical about two Japanese American siblings at an internment camp during WWII. The role was created with Salonga in mind and she had been involved with the production since its developmental phase in '08. She has been cast as Erzulie, the goddess of love, for the 2017 Broadway revival of the musical "Once on This Island."

Georgina Pazcoguin was cast as Victoria in the Broadway production of "Cats" in 2016. Pazcoguin was born in Altoona, Pennsylvania, joined the New York City Ballet in '01, and was promoted in '13 as the company's first Asian American soloist. She made her Broadway debut as Ivy Smith in the musical "On The Town" ('14). Also in 2016, Karla Garcia, born in Oxon Hill, Maryland, was cast as a female swing in the Broadway production of the musical "Hamilton." A swing learns several different roles and takes the place of absent cast members during a show's run.

In 2016, Ali Ewoldt became the first Asian American to play Christine Daae in "Phantom of the Opera" on Broadway since it opened in 1988 at Majestic Theatre. Ewoldt, whose mother is Filipino, was born in the Chicago area. "Being the first Asian American Christine on Broadway is an honor

---

[66] Ang. "Lea Salonga, back on Broadway: 'There has been zero video game time for me.'" *PDI*. Oct. 26, 2015.

and, also, I believe, comes with a bit of responsibility," she said. "I want to demonstrate that this incredible story can be told regardless of my personal ethnic background.

"Growing up Filipino, music was always a part of my family gatherings. My Aunt Myrna took me to some of my first Broadway shows and my parents continued that tradition when they realized how much I loved watching them. My parents were always incredibly supportive, shuttling me to dance classes and voice lessons, etc."[67] Ewoldt made her Broadway debut in '06 as Cosette during the revival run of "Les Miserables" where she was able to share the stage with Salonga when the latter was cast as Fantine in '07.

Eva Noblezada, Jon Jon Briones, and Devin Ilaw have been cast as Kim, the Engineer, and Thuy, respectively, for the 2017-18 revival of "Miss Saigon," with Lianah Sta. Ana as Kim alternate and Billy Bustamante as Engineer alternate.

Clint Ramos (1974–) received the 2016 Tony Award for Best Costume Design in a Play for his work on African American Danai Gurira's "Eclipsed," about five women's struggles during the second Liberian Civil War. Ramos' work was described by critics as "meticulously detailed" (Variety), "evocative" (Hollywood Reporter), "[takes] much research, labor, and talent to pull off," (Vanityfair.com) and "essential" (Vogue.com).

His costumes combined traditional African fabrics like lapa (woven cotton cloth with colorful patterns) and T-shirts emblazoned with American pop-culture images such as

---

[67] Ang. "Fil-Am Ali Ewoldt is first Asian to play Christine in 'Phantom of the Opera' on Broadway." *PDI*. Aug. 27, 2016.

"Rugrats" cartoon characters (to show that Liberia is a repository for American discards). Some characters were given brand-name footwear to show status.

Ramos researched photographs of the war and sourced shirts and fabrics from vintage clothing shops and African merchandise stores in New York. Copies of ready-to-wear tops and bottoms that were chosen for the production were recreated from scratch: shirts were silkscreened and jeans were tailored to accommodate the rigors of being used multiple shows a week and to fit different cast members. The costumes were then distressed, treated with dyes to mimic sweat or blood stains that could not be washed off when the costumes were laundered.

His other credits include costume designs for "Here Lies Love," where critics lauded his work as "vast and fabulous" (New York Times), "[providing] beautiful symmetry" (Hollywood Reporter), and "top-notch" (New York Magazine). Ramos previously received the 2013 Obie Award for Sustained Excellence of Costume Design.

Born and raised in Cebu, Ramos moved to the US in 1993 to take a master's in Design for Stage and Film at NYU's Tisch School of the Arts on a full scholarship. He has since designed costumes and sets for over a hundred productions in New York, across the US, and internationally.[68]

---

[68] Ang. "Dulaang UP's Clint Ramos wins Tony for costume design." *PDI.* Jun. 14, 2016.

Acknowledgments

My thanks,

To everyone who reports on and writes about theater.

To all the theater makers (or their family members) who were patient and gracious with my unending questions and were equally generous with their stories. To everyone who extended a hand whenever they encountered my many pleas for help during the preparation of this book.

To Giselle Garcia and Jozza Palaganas, for inputs. To Lady Santelices, for the able hand. To Jaclyn Lutanco, for the sharp eye.

To Rene Ciria-Cruz and Esther Chavez, of Inquirer.net's USA and Canada Section. To Cora Llamas, Gibbs Cadiz, and Vincen Yu, colleagues and friends from Philippine Daily Inquirer's Theater Section.

To the Muñozes: Grace, Lourdes, and Cynthia. To Carmen Ong-Lim, who has always told me I would write a book one day. To the Angs of Chino Hills: Lambert, Lulu, and Melissa.

To Myra Fong, Jo Robles, my ESS Raven Ong, and my BFF Ronald Elepano, for friendship and laughter.

To my late mother Betty Ong and my father Zeldo "Tom" Ang, who has raised and loved me and my siblings single-handedly for many years. To my siblings, Melody Jane and Clark Velayo, John Ronald, and Thomas Ryan, zot!

To Constantine Dy, for everything and more.

References,
readings, resources

References

In print edition, selected references are cited in footnotes. In ebook edition, citations may appear as endnotes.

Readings

Selected publications listed below have been helpful in providing information for this book and are suggested for further reading.

Filipino American theater

"Stage Presence: Conversations with Filipino American Performing Artists" Edited by Theodore Gonzalves. Meritage Press, 2007.

Includes interviews with Reme Grefalda, Jessica Hagedorn, Allan Manalo, Ralph Peña.

"Savage Stage: Plays by Ma-Yi Theater Company" Edited by Joi Barrios-Leblanc. Ma-Yi Theater Company, 2007.
Introduction includes history of the company. Includes plays by Filipino Americans or with Filipino American subject matter: Lonnie Carter's "The Romance of Magno Rubio," Linda Faigao-Hall's "Woman From The Other Side of the World," Chris Millado's "peregriNasyon," Han Ong's "Middle Finger," Ong and Sung Rno's "Savage Acts," Ralph Peña's "Flipzoids," and Peña and Rno's "Project: Balangiga."

"The Day the Dancers Stayed" By Theodore Gonzalves. Temple University Press, 2009.

"Puro Arte: Filipinos on the Stages of Empire" By Lucy Mae San Pablo Burns. New York University Press, 2012.

Profiles of Filipino American playwrights
"Unbroken Thread: An Anthology of Plays by Asian American Women" Roberta Uno, ed. University of Massachusetts Press, 1993.
*Includes an entry on Jeannie Barroga.
Also includes Barroga's "Walls."*

"Asian American Playwrights: A Bio-Bibliographical Critical Sourcebook" Miles Xian Liu, ed. Greenwood Press, 2002.
Includes entries on Jeannie Barroga, Louella Dizon, Linda Faigao-Hall, Jessica Hagedorn, Paul Stephen Lim, Han Ong, Ralph Peña.

Filipino American history
"The Filipino Americans from 1763 to the present: Their history, culture, and traditions" By Veltisezar Bautista. Bookhaus Publishers, 1998.

"The Filipino Americans" By Barbara Mercedes Posadas. Greenwood Press, 1999; Second edition 2002.

Philippine theater
"A Short History of Philippine Theater" Edited by Isagani Cruz. Cultural Center of the Philippines, 1971.

"Encyclopedia of Philippine Art" Editor-in-chief: Nicanor Tiongson. Cultural Center of the Philippines, 1994. Second edition, forthcoming in 2018.

"Palabas: Essays on Philippine Theater History" By Doreen Fernandez. Ateneo de Manila University Press, 1996.

Philippine history
"History of the Philippines: From Indios Bravos to Filipinos" By Luis Francia. Overlook Press, 2010.

Asian American theater
"A History of Asian American Theatre History" By Esther Kim Lee. Temple University Press, 2006.

Resources

Online resources
Facebook.com/groups/FilipinoAmericanTheater   is   a Facebook group for Filipino American Theater where artists, groups, and theatergoers are welcome to join to monitor or post announcements on upcoming shows, workshops, auditions, etc.

It is always possible for website addresses or URLs (uniform resource locator) to change. It's best to do online searches for Filipino American theater companies to access their current address. However, if searching for older versions of existing or defunct sites, Archive.org's Wayback Machine is a useful tool.

Roger Tang's Asian American Theater Revue site is a useful clearinghouse of news and information on Asian American theater.

Contacting playwrights
Some Filipino American playwrights have agents and some can be contacted directly for permissions and arrangements to stage their work.

Some Filipino American playwrights have listed their works on Doollee.com or NewPlayExchange.org.

Anthologies with plays by Filipino Americans
"Between Worlds: Contemporary Asian-American Plays" Misha Berson, ed. Theatre Communications Group, 1990.
Includes Jessica Hagedorns' "Tenement Lover."

"Contemporary Plays by Women of Color" Kathy Perkins and Roberta Uno, eds. Routledge, 1996.
Includes Louella Dizon's "Till Voices Wake Us."

"But Still, Like Air, I'll Rise: New Asian American Plays" Velina Hasu Houston, ed. Temple University Press, 1997.
Includes Jeannie Barroga's "Talk Story."

"Tokens? The NYC Asian American Experience On Stage" Alvin Eng, ed. The Asian American Writers' Workshop, 1999.
Includes Jessica Hagedorn's "Silent Movie," Han Ong's "Swoony Planet," Ralph Peña's "Flipzoids," and Gary San Angel's "The Right Stuff."

"Yellow Light: The Flowering of Asian American Arts"
Amy Ling, ed. Temple University Press, 1999.
Includes "No Menus Please" from "Big Dicks, Asian Men," and "Diary of a Paper Son" from "The Second Coming;" both by Slant Performance Group.

"Monologues for Actors of Color" Roberta Uno, ed.
Routledge, 2016.
Includes Francis Tanglao-Aguas' "The Sarimanok Travels."

Publications of plays by Filipino Americans
Clarence Coo
"Removing the Glove" Baker's Plays, 1994.
"Bahala na (Let It Go)" University Press, 2011.
"Beautiful Province" Yale Drama Series, 2013.

Linda Faigao-Hall
"The Female Heart and Other Plays" NoPassport Press,
    2013.
    (Includes: The Female Heart; Woman From the Other
    Side of the World; God, Sex, and Blue Water; and State
    Without Grace).

Michael Golamco
"Cowboy Versus Samurai" Samuel French, 2011.
"Year Zero" Samuel French, 2011.

Jessica Hagedorn
"Dogeaters" Theatre Communications Group, 2002.

*Justin Jain (and Dave Johnson, Brian McCann, Tim Sawicki,
Bradley Wrenn)*
"The Very Merry Xmas Carol Holiday Adventure Show"
    Playscripts, 2000

Paul Stephen Lim
"Conpersonas" Samuel French, 1977.
"Woeman" Aran Press, 1985.
"Report to the River" One Act Play Depot, 2002.

A. Rey Pamatmat
"A Spare Me" Playscripts, 2000.
"Thunder Above, Deeps Below" Samuel French, 2012.
"Edith Can Shoot Things and Hit Them" Samuel French,
    2012.

Jorshinelle Taleon-Sonza
"Dogs Days in America" Central Books, 2012.
        (Includes: Dog Days in America; How to Cook
        Adobo; First Night; Woman of Oz; Sandman; Cold
        Flesh; and Pure)
"Haiyan and Other Plays about the Homeland" University
    of the Philippines Press, 2016.
        (Includes: Haiyan; The Encounter; Lena's Way; and
        The Passion of Andres B.)

Index

In the ebook edition, using the "search" function is recommended for finding mentions of index entries within the book.

25th Annual Putnam County Spelling Bee, The, 117
90 in the Shade, 10
  Bolton, Guy, 10
  Kern, Jerome, 10
  Smith, Harry, 10
A Contemporary Theatre, 20
  Multicultural Playwrights Festival, 20
Abad, Ricaro "Ricky", 36
Abad-Cardinalli, Marilyn, 78
Abuba, Ernest Hawkins, 67, 116
  American Story, An, 68
  Dowager, The, 68
  Eat a Bowl of Tea, 68
Academy of Ballet (San Francisco), 145
Acting Company, The (John Houseman), 110
Actor's Stage Studio, 67
Actors' Equity Association, 15, 42, 102, 127, 155
Acuña, Arthur, 126
Adams, Neile, 39
  Arrastia, Ruby Salvador, 39
  Salvador, Carmen "Miami", 39
Ade, George, 9
  Sultan of Sulu, 9, 10
Adiarte, Patrick, 39
Adrales, May, 160
African, 13, 129
African American, 10, 16, 38, 43, 44, 55, 59, 83, 105, 136, 149, 159, 169
Agana, Marcelino, 35, 119
  New Yorker in Tondo, 35, 119
Aguillon, Michelle, 157
Aguinaldo, Emilio, 5, 7
Alaska, 14, 18, 19, 20, 23, 63, 157
Albalos, Mario, 53
  Adda Lunod Dagti Pasamak [*Tragic Events*], 53
  Nailet ti Lubong [*The World is Small*], 53
  Nasutil ti Lubong [*The World is*

Unpredictable], 53
Albuquerque, New Mexico, 79
Alejandro, Reynaldo "Ronnie", 56, 115
  Reynaldo Alejandro Dance Theater, 115
Alexandria, Virginia, 138
Alforque, Alcide "Sonny", 141
Alitaptap Filipino Dance Troupe [Firefly Filipino Dance Troupe], 158
All Nations Dance Company, 115
Allegiance, 168
Almedilla, Joan, 71
Altoona, Pennsylvania, 168
Alvarez, Boni, 155
  Bloodletting, 156
  Dallas Non-Stop, 156
  Ruby Tragically Rotund, 156
Alves, Anna, 134
Alvin Ailey American Dance Center, 85
Amador, Zenaida, 46
  International Visitors Program, 46
  New York Academy of Dramatic Arts, 46
  University of South Dakota, 46
America is in the Heart, 24, 100
America is in the Heart (book), 23, 24, 58, 100
American Academy of Dramatic Art, 58
American College Theatre Festival, 66, 79
American Conservatory Theater, 25, 62, 64, 108
American Musical and Dramatic Academy, 137
American Place Theatre, 48
American Repertory Theater, 106
American Theatre Magazine, 127
amusement parks, 14
Ang Mundo ay Isang Mansanas [*The World is An Apple*], 119
Ang Pagpapaamo sa Maldita [*Taming of the Shrew*], 36

Antero (Cabrera, Antero), 13
Antoine, Andre, 15
Apostol, Rinabeth, 69
Aquino Jr., Benigno "Ninoy", 71, 83, 84
Aquino, Corazon "Cory", 71, 83
Arab American, 59, 144
Aranas, Raul, 116
Arcenas, Loy, 94, 96, 97, 126
Arena Stage, 96
Arizona Commission on the Arts, 54
Artigiani Troupe, 151
artistic director, 46, 47, 55, 58, 62, 84,
    86, 93, 106, 109, 113, 120, 127, 131,
    132, 133, 136, 137, 144, 147, 149,
    150, 151, 157, 158, 159, 160, 163,
    164
Ashland, Oregon, 136
Asian American, 43, 149
    actors, 14, 44, 64, 82, 87, 102, 159
    actors' training, 62
    as a category for plays, 67
    experience, 96, 128
    identity, 44, 64
    playwrights, 127, 128, 137
    representation, 164
    theater awareness, 76
    theater dynamics, 61
    theater group, 2, 95, 112, 153
    theater makers, 79, 116, 121, 149
Asian American Political Alliance, 44
Asian American Theater Company, 44,
    49, 62, 79, 81, 82, 133
    Asian American Theater
        Workshop, 62, 64
Asian Arts Initiative, 113
Asian Exclusion Act. See Northwest
    Asian American Theatre
Asian Multi Media Center (AMMC), 60
    Chin, Douglas, 60
    Filipino Youth Activities, 60
Asian Stories in America, 121
    Kang, Stan, 121
Asis, Stan, 23, 51, 61
    Monkey King The Transformation,
        62
    Philippine Legends Folklore and
        American Impressions, 23, 61
    Pinoy Lot, The, 51
Assassins, 99
Association for Theatre in Higher
    Education, 151
Ateneo de Manila, 30, 36, 45, 47
    Ateneo Experimental Theater, 45
    Ateneo Graduate Summer Drama
        Program, 47

Ateneo Players' Guild, 30
Tanghalang Ateneo, 36
Ating Tao [Our People], 49
Alfonso, Rosalie, 50
    Coconut, 50
    Luis, Benny, 51
    Marcos, Don, 51
    Syquia, Serafin, 50
Award
    American Book Award, 108
    Drama Desk Award, 126
    George Jean Nathan Award, 127
    Laurence Olivier Award, 102
    Lilly Award, 127
    Michael Merritt Award for
        Excellence in Design and
        Collaboration, 99
    National Student Playwriting
        Award, 66
    Obie Award, 42, 68, 71, 97, 115, 126,
        127, 170
    Paul Stephen Lim Asian American
        Playwriting Award, 128
    Rosetta LeNoire Award, 127
    Seidman Award for Excellence in
        Design, 97
    Tony Award, 41, 76, 103, 166, 169
    Yale Drama Series Award, 139
Bacalzo, Dan, 113
    I'm Sorry But I Don't Speak the
        Language, 113
Bacling, Andres, 21
Bagong Diwa [New Essence] (dance
    group), 63, 91
Bahaghari Productions [Rainbow
    Productions], 119
    Tatluhang Dula [Three Plays], 119
Baker, George Pierce, 78
Baker, Paul, 47
Baltazar, Gabe, 21
barangay, 1, 129
Barnsdall Theater, 130
Barnum and Bailey Circus, 12
Barrios, Sister Angela, 56
    Hello Soldier, 56
Barroga, Jeannie, 81, 83, 89, 92
    Abend, Judith, 82
    Buffalo'ed, 83
    Eye of the Coconut, 82
    Kenny Was A Shortstop, 83
    Pigeon Man, The, 81
    Reaching for the Stars, 82
    Rita's Resources, 83
    Talk Story, 83
    Walls, 83

Barrows, David, 11
Basic Integrated Theater Arts
    Workshop, 91
Batayola, Maria, 61, 62
    Gathering Ground, 62
    Love Sutras, 62
    Wong, Chris, 62
Battle of Manila, 5
Bayanihan Dance Company, 73, 111,
    118
    Benitez, Helena, 73
    Brussels World's Fair, 74
    Ed Sullivan Show, The, 74
    Kasilag, Lucrecia, 74
    Urtula, Lucrecia, 73
bearded ladies, 13
Benjamin Pimentel, 27
Bernardino, Eduardo "Edu.", 121
Berserker Residents, 148
    Annihilation Point, 148
    Giant Squid, The, 148
    Jersey Devil, 148
    Johnson, David, 148
    Wrenn, Bradley, 148
Bijou Theater, 10
Bindlestiff Studio, 24, 27, 74, 76, 132,
    139, 140, 162
    Dorado, Michael, 29
    Gravador, Rhoda, 29
    Icban, Joshua, 29
    Love Edition, The, 140
    Pinoy Midsummer, A, 163
    Plaza Apartments, 133
    Plaza Hotel, 132
    Stories High, 140
    Tagalog A Festival of One-Acts, 162
blackface, 16
Blaney, Charles, 9
    Across the Pacific, 9
bodabil, 16, 23, 37
Bontoc, 13, See also Igorot
Borromeo, Luis, 16
Boston, 106
Boy Scouts, 12
Braganza, Miguel, 84
Brahm, Otto, 15
Brecht, Bertolt, 64, 96
    Caucasian Chalk Circle, 68, 96
    In the Jungle of Cities, 64
Bridgeport, Connecticut, 30
Bridgewater, New Jersey, 138
Brill, Robert, 98
Briones, Jon Jon, 169
Broadway
    industry, 1, 14, 38, 41, 76, 94, 125,
        165
    production, 14, 16, 23, 33, 38, 67, 68,
        76, 77, 97, 99, 102, 116, 117, 145,
        165
Broadway Barkada [Broadway
    Clique], 136
Brooke, Peter, 58
Brown University, 157, 161
Brustein, Robert, 106
B-Side Productions, 137
Buell, Evangeline, 79
    Twenty Five Chickens and a Pig for
        a Bride Growing Up in a Filipino
        Immigrant Family (book), 79
Buffalo, New York, 8
Bulosan, Carlos, 23, 61
Burns, Lucy Mae San Pablo, 3, 134, 135
Bustamante, Billy, 136, 169
Butiu, Melody, 55, 71
Cabico, Regie, 113
Cachapero, Emilya, 50, 63, 68
Caldwell Playhouse (Caldwell Theatre
    Company), 97
California
    Alameda, 64
    Fairfield, 167
    Half Moon Bay, 167
    Hayward, 158
    Monterey, 122, 141
    Palo Alto, 82, 155
    Salinas, 99
    San Jose, 78
    Stockton, 22
California State University
    Hayward, 78
    Los Angeles, 48
    Sacramento, 141
Calud, Annette, 104
Cambodian American, 153
Campo Santo, 114
    Hall, Margo, 114
    Saguar, Luis, 114
    Torres, Michael, 114
Candido, Romeo, 162
Carlsbad Playhouse, 143
Carnegie Institute of Technology
    (Carnegie Mellon University), 78
Carrillo, Cely, 40, 68
Carter, Lonnie, 24, 126
Carvajal, Celina "Lena Hall", 166
Casasola, Elizabeth "Liz", 71, 136
Catholic University of America, 119
Cats, 68, 76, 117, 166, 168
Cebu, 170
Cebu City, 80

Center Theatre Group, 99, 152
Cervantes, Benjamin "Behn", 45, 110
    Beloit College, 45
Chalk Repertory Theatre, 148
Chang, Jennifer, 148
Chang, Tisa, 67
Chehlaoui, Maha, 144
Chekhov, Anton, 119
    Marriage Proposal, The, 119
Chess, 104
Chicago, 10, 14, 24, 59, 76, 86, 99, 101,
    121, 132, 139, 165, 168
Chin, Frank, 48, 62, 66
    Chickencoop Chinaman, The, 48
Chinese American, 23, 38, 48, 60, 61,
    67, 76, 87, 112
Chinese nightclubs, 22
    Chinese Sky Room, 22
    Forbidden City, 22
Chorus Line, A, 39, 68
Cinderella, 77
CIRCA-Pintig (Pintig Cultural Group),
    24, 76, 86, 99, 144, 150
    Aliposa, Levi, 100
    Belen, Rey, 100
    Belen, Riza, 100
    Calo, Divina, 100
    Castro, Daisy, 100
    Clarito, Jerry, 100
    Gaston, Andy, 134
    Gonzalez-Kirpach, Susan, 100
    Leopoldo, Ginger, 100
    Mascarenas, Ramon, 100
    Ramos, Edessa, 100
    Reyes, Jimi, 100
    Sargan, Allan, 100
City College of San Francisco, 79
Clown School (Los Angeles), 151
    Bridel, David, 151
Colendrino, Filomena, 119
    Why Women Wash the Dishes, 119
College of William and Mary, 131, 138
colonization
    by Spain, 1, 5, 8, 36
    by USA, 2, 36
    colonial government, 7, 8, 11, 12, 14
    colonial mentality, 34
Columbia University, 45, 138, 145
comedy, 129, *See also* komedya
comedy, 10, 35, 39, 65, 68, 83, 140, 155
    satire, 9, 34, 51, 74
commedia dell'arte, 140, 151
community theater, 15, 18, 29, 64
Consortium of Asian American
    Theaters and Artists, 136

Coo, Clarence, 138
    Bahala Na (Let It Go), 139
    Beautiful Province, 139
    People Sitting in Darkness, 139
    Proof Through the Night, 138
Coon, Hilton, 6
    Under the American Flag, 6
Cordova, Dorothy, 60
Cordova, Fred, 60
Cordova, Lucia "Lucing", 22, 61
    Accompanado, Sally, 22
    Cruz, Raymundo, 22
    *Walang Kamatayang Pagibig [Love
        Eternal],* 22
Cordova, Timoteo "Tim", 60, 109
    Across Oceans of Dreams, 109
    Bamboo Split, 110
    Barkada Syndrome, 110
    Heart of the Son, 110
    Makisig, 61
Corpuz, Jon Viktor, 167
costume design, 97, 121
county fairs, 14
Covington, Virginia, 160
Criss, Darren, 166
Cruz-Arantea, Gemma, 61
    Makisig The little hero of Mactan
        (book), 61
Cultural Center of the Philippines, 3,
    55, 85, 95
    Philippine Rehabilitation Act of
        1946, 55
Cunanan, Andrew, 109
Current Theatrics, 150
    Costello, Thomas, 150
Daguio, Amador, 56
    Wedding Dance (story), 56
Dallas Theater Center, 47
Damn Yankees, 68, 159
Damon and Pythias, 30
Dang, Tim, 136
Davao City, 31, 84
De Castro, Thelma Virata, 142
    Goddess of Flowers, The, 143
    Meet the Family, 143
De Jesus, Carmen, 162
De La Cruz, Alison, 156
    Naturally Graceful, 156
    Sungka, 156
De la Cruz, Catalina "Katy", 23
De la Cruz, Edgardo, 78
    Directing for Theater A Personal
        Approach (book), 79
De La Cruz, Juan, 12
De La Cruz, Martina, 12

De Leon, Luz, 86, 88, 92, 93
De Leon, Reggie, 167
De los Angeles, Servando, 119
    Ang Kiri [The Coquette], 119
De Ocampo, Ramon, 126
Depression, Great, 17, 123
Desipina & Co., 138
Dickens, Charles, 81
Discovery Project, 82
discrimination, 18, 128, 154
    anti-miscegenation, 25
    Civil Rights Act (1964), 43
Disney's Aladdin, 167
Disney's Beauty and the Beast, 76, 104
Disney's The Lion King, 76, 104
Diverse City Theater Company, 81,
    137, 145, 154
    Kern, Maxine, 146
Diwa [Essence] (artist collective), 63
Dizon, Louella, 93
    Till Voices Wake Us, 93
dog eating, 13
Dogeaters, 69, 108
Dogeaters (book), 70
Domingo, Jr., Nemesio, 51, 60
    Ameria, 51
Domingo, Ron, 126
drama festival (University of Hawaii)
    Ilocano, 52
    Tagalog, 80
Dramatic Compositions Copyrighted in
    the United States 1870 to 1916
    (book), 11
Dramatists Guild, 128
Dulaan ng mga Tao [Theater of the
    People], 51
dwarves, 13
East West Players, 24, 44, 47, 64, 70,
    136, 143, 148, 152, 156
    Creevey, Rae, 47
    David Henry Hwang Theater, 70
    David Henry Hwang Writer's
        Institute, 143, 156
    Hong, James, 47
    Iwamatsu, Makoto "Mako", 47, 64
    Johnson, Glenn, 49
    Kim, June, 47
    Lee, Guy, 47
    Li, Pat, 48
    Lock, Yet, 48
    Quo, Beulah, 48
    Tales of Juan and Taro, 49
    Theater for Youth Program, 148
    Urashima Taro, 49
education system, 11, 32

Ells, Chrystene, 123
Encyclopedia of Philippine Art, 3
English Alternative Theatre, 80
English National Opera, 97
Escueta, Melvyn "Mel", 62
    Honey Bucket, 62
Espiritu, Prescila "Precy", 52
Estados Unidos versus Juan Matapang
    Cruz [United States versus Juan
    Matapang Cruz], 46
Estrada, Ariel, 149
Ethnic Cultural Center Theater, 51, 61
Ethnic Studies, 44, 49, 57, 73
ethnic theater, 44
Eusebio, Nelson, 150
Ewoldt, Ali, 168
Exchange Visitor Program (nurses), 26
Exposition
    1904 World's Fair (see Louisiana
        Purchase), 12
    Alaska Yukon Pacific, 14
    Filipino American Arts, 92
    Greater America, 7
    Jamestown, 14
    Lewis and Clark Centennial, 14
    Louisiana Purchase, 12, 36, 86, 92,
        100
    Pan American, 8
    Panama-Pacific International, 16
    Philippine Reservation, 13
    Philippine Village, 6, 7
    St. Louis World's Fair (see
        Louisiana Purchase), 12
    Trans Mississippi and
        International, 6
Fagen, David, 83
Faigao-Hall, Linda Kalayaan, 80, 82,
    126, 146, 154
    Bretton Hall College (England), 80
    Cornelio Faigao Memorial Annual
        Writer's Workshop, 81
    Female Heart and Other Plays
        (book), 81
    Female Heart, The, 146
    State without Grace, 81, 82
    Woman From The Other Side of the
        World, 126
Fajilan, Ann, 79, 92
    Seven Card Stud with Seven
        Manangs Wild, 79
    Twenty Five Chickens and a Pig, 79
Federal Theatre Project, 17
Fernandez, Doreen, 3, 32, 34
Festival of American Playwrights of
    Color, 79

Filipinescas Dance Company, 115
Filipiniana (roving troupe), 118
Filipino American
    characters in plays or musicals, 49,
        56, 62, 63, 67, 68, 69, 81, 82, 83,
        86, 90, 93, 107, 109, 117, 121,
        139, 142, 143, 146, 147, 154, 156,
        158
    experience, 94
    identity, 50, 51, 73, 76, 147
    portraying other ethnicities, 22, 38,
        67, 104, 116, 129, 167
Filipino American National Historical
    Society, 61
Filipino Art Lovers Club, 21
    Punahou Music School scholarship,
        21
Filipino Canadian, 162
Filipino Carnival (Stockton), 22
Filipino Catholic Club Drama Guild, 19
Filipino Club (California State
    University
    Sacramento), 141
Filipino Student Association
    (University of Washington), 61
film
    adapted for, 39
    adapted from, 35, 76
    working in, 40, 59, 77, 103
Fitch, Clyde, 9
    Her Own Way, 9
Flanagan, Hallie, 17
Flipzoids, 62, 93, 96, 115, 122, 126, 161
Flor, Balatazar "Bob" Fernandez, 19
    Eve of the Fiesta of St. Vincent de
        Ferrer, The, 19
    Retribution, 19
Flor, Robert Francis Fernandez, 19
    My Uncle's Letters, 20
Florida, 148, 167
Florida Gulf Coast University, 114
Flower Drum Song, 23, 38, 39, 40, 103,
    117
Ford Foundation, 42, 134
Fordham University, 30
Fraser, John, 6
    Dewey the hero of Manila, 6
Freehold Theater, 20
Fritz Theatre, 143
    Fritz Blitz of New Plays by
        California Writers, 143
Gamalinda, Eric, 146
    Resurrection, 146
Garcia, Karla, 168
Garrot Edades, Jean, 31, 32

Edades, Victorio, 31
    More Short Plays of the Philippines
        (book), 31
    Onstage and Offstage (book), 31
    Short Plays of the Philippines
        including Advice for the
        amateur director (book), 31
Gavilan College, 78
Geary Theater, 64
Gener, Randy, 127
    University of Nevada-Reno, 128
Generator Theater Company, 157
George Mason University, 151
Georgetown University, 131
Gilbert, William Schwenck, 30, 75
Gilroy, California, 78
Giuliani, Rudolph, 125
Glass Menagerie, The, 97
Godspell, 168
Godspell on Broadway Cast of 2032,
    167
Golamco, Michael, 131, 152
    Achievers, 152
    Build, 153
    Cowboy Versus Samurai, 131, 153
    Year Zero, 153
Gonzalez, Jojo, 126
Gonzalves, Theodore, 134, 135
    Day the Dancers Stayed, The
        (book), 135
    Stage Presence Conversations with
        Filipino American Performing
        Artists (book), 135
Goodman Theatre, 99
Gotanda, Philip Kan, 25
Goucher College, 154
Grand Opera House (New York City),
    10
Grape Strike, 25
    Chavez, Cesar, 25
    Itliong, Larry, 24
    Vera Cruz, Philip, 25
Great White Way, 15
Green Room Series, 146
Grefalda, Reme-Antonia, 120, 134
    30 December 1896, 121
    In the Matter of Willie Grayson, 121
    Mama, Mama, Do We Have
        Rehearsals Tonite?, 121
    Who Sez I'm A Coconut?, 121
Greif, Michael, 109
Guerrero, Wilfrido, 34
    Wow! These Americans, 34
guerrilla theater, 51
Guidote-Alvarez, Cecile, 47, 55, 116,

120
Alvarez, Heherson "Sonny", 55
State University of New York-
    Albany, 47
GUMIL Hawaii (Gunglo Dagiti
    Mannurat nga Ilokano iti Hawaii)
    [Association of Ilocano Writers in
    Hawaii], 52
Gurira, Danai, 169
    Eclipsed, 169
Gus Solomons Jr. Dance Company, 112
Guthrie Theater, 159
Gutierrez, Gabrielle "Gabby", 168
Guys and Dolls, 99
Habito, D., 119
    Panhik Ligaw, 119
Hagedorn, Jessica Tarahata, 69, 107,
    108, 114, 116
    Fe in the Desert, 114
    Gangster Choir, The (band), 108
    Mango Tango, 108
    Most Wanted, 109
    Stairway to Heaven, 114
    Surrender, 108
    Tenement Lover, 108
Hall, Cliffton, 104
Hall, Juanita, 38
Hall, Lena. See Carvajal, Celina
Hamilton, 168
Hammerstein II, Oscar, 30, 37, 77
Hampton Roads, Virginia, 14
Harvard University, 78, 85, 155
Harvey, Dave. See McTurk, David
    Harvey
Hawaii, 18, 20, 26, 45, 52, 53, 59, 67, 78,
    80, 83, 85, 102, 104, 110, 111, 151,
    160
Hawaii Alliance for Performing Arts,
    111
    Acosta, Neric, 111
    Coronel, John, 111
    Lucila Lalu, 111
Hawaii Alliance for Philippine
    Performing Arts, 111
Hedwig and the Angry Inch, 166
Here Lies Love, 55, 71, 166, 167, 170
    Byrne, David, 71
    Cook, Norman "Fatboy Slim", 71
Hernandez, Tomas, 53
    Estrella, 53
Highways Performance Space, 106
Holy City Zoo, 122
Houseman, John, 110
Houston, Whitney, 77
Hovey Players, 157

How the Grinch Stole Christmas, 168
How to Succeed in Business Without
    Really Trying, 166
HT Chen and Dancers, 112
Hwang, David Henry, 76, 103, 116
    Golden Child, 77
    M. Butterfly, 76
Igorot, 12, 13, 86, 100
    Filipino Exhibition Company, 14
    Hunt, Truman, 13
    Igorot Exhibit Company, 13
    Igorrote (spelling), 12
    Schneidewind, Richard, 14
Ilaw, Devin, 169
Imelda A New Musical, 70, 72, 136
    Coleman, Aaron, 70
    Del Mundo, Liza, 70
    Diel, Antoine, 71
    Maghuyop, Mel Sagrado, 71
    Ocenar, Myra Cris, 71
    Oyama, Sachi, 70
    Wang, Nathan, 70
Immigration legislation
    Asian Exclusion Act (1924), 17
    Asiatic Barred Zone Act (1917), 17
    Chinese Exclusion Act (1882), 17
    Gentlemen's Agreement (1907), 17
    Immigration and Nationality Act
        (1965), 43
    Luce-Celler Act (1946), 26
    Page Act (1875), 17
    War Brides Act (1945), 26
In The Heights, 167
independence (country)
    Philippines, 5, 26
    USA, 17
Indiana University, 137
Indonesian American, 157
International Centre for Theatre
    Research, 58
International Hotel, 25
International Performance Arts
    eXchange (College of William and
    Mary), 131
International Theatre Institute, 56, 64
internment camp, 30, 33, 168
Intersection for the Arts, 114
InTheater Magazine, 113
IRA (Irish Republican Army), 59
Irish American, 6, 150
Irwin, Henry Lee, 30
Isaac, Alberto, 48, 63
    Coda, 49, 63
    How Juan Found His Fortune, 49
Jackson, Michael, 162

Thriller (song), 162
Jacobs, Adam, 167
Jacobs, Arielle, 167
Jain, Justin, 148
Japanese American, 25, 49, 61, 112, 113, 168
Joaquin, Nick, 78, 118, 119
  May Day Eve, 119
  Portrait of the Artist as Filipino, A, 78, 118
Joaquin, Sarah, 118
  Far Eastern University (FEU) Drama Guild, 118
  Of Laughter and Tears (book), 119
John F. Kennedy Center for the Performing Arts, 66, 80, 128
Jose, Brian, 71, 136
Juan, Anton, 131
  Centre Universitaire International de Formation et des Recherches Dramatiques [International University Center for Training and Dramatic Research], 132
Juan, Joyce, 29, 123
Juilliard School, The, 40, 96, 110, 151, 159, 161
Julia Miles Theatre, 71
Kamatayan ng Isang Duwag [Death of a Coward], 119
Kansas City, 80
Kasla Gloria Ti Hawaii [Hawaii is Like Paradise], 110
Katigbak, Maria Corazon "Mia", 87, 95, 116, 127, 136, 164
  Reyes, Adelaida, 88
Katipunan ng mga Demokratikong Pilipino (KDP) [Union of Democratic Filipinos], 57
Kennedy Theater (Honolulu), 85
Kenyon College, 131
Kilos Sining [Movement Arts], 117
  Brooks, George, 118
  Morales, Nicky, 118
  Morales-Encarnacion, Angelina "Leni", 118
  Payongayong, Ellen, 118
  Simbulan, Teresa, 118
  Simon, Romel, 118
  Victoria, Art, 118
  Villorante, Munam, 118
Kinding Sindaw [Dance of Light], 118
King and I, The, 38, 39, 116, 117, 145, 167
  Brynner, Yul, 38
  Watanabe, Ken, 117

Kinky Boots, 166
Kirk Douglas Theater, 69
Kismet, 39
komedya, 129
Korean American, 121
Kulintang Arts, 60, 91, 147
Kulintang Ensemble, 91
Kultura (dance group), 167
Kumu Kahua Theater, 151
kundiman, 92
La Jolla Playhouse, 69, 99, 109
La MaMa Experimental Theatre Club, 55, 56, 68, 97, 108, 112, 115, 152
labor union, 15
laborers, 17, 18, 23, 24, 25, 86, 109, 159
Lacson, Chuck, 140
Lagrimas, Arlene, 22
Lagrimas, Gonzalo Anthony, 23
Lagundino, Flordelino, 150, 157
Lapeña-Bonifacio, Amelia, 61
  Short Short Life of Citizen Juan, The, 61
Lapu the Coyote that Cares Theatre Company (University of California Los Angeles), 153
Larawan [Portrait], 118
Lark Play Development Center, 161
Las Vegas, 150
Latin American, 25, 43, 44, 59, 114, 136, 149, 159
League of Resident Theatres, 43
Lee, Esther Kim, 3
  History of Asian American Theatre, A (book), 3
Les Miserables, 76, 103, 117, 167, 169
Leviathan Lab, 149, 155, 158
Library of Congress, 54, 132
Likha Pilipino Folk Ensemble [Create Pilipino Folk Ensemble], 86
Likha Promotions [Create Promotions], 86, 90
Lim, Paul Stephen, 49, 63, 66, 80, 128
  Conpersonas, 66
  Flesh, Flash and Frank Harris, 66
  Mother Tongue, 66
  Points of Departure, 63, 66
  Woeman, 66
Lim, Rafael "Raf", 140
Lincoln Center, 167
Lirio, Victor, 145, 154
  Dempster, Curt, 146
  Ensemble Studio Theatre, 146
literary manager, 48, 83, 143
Little Theater movement, 15
Llana, Jose, 55, 71, 116, 162, 167

Lopez, Robert, 166
    Avenue Q, 166
    Book of Mormon, 166
Los Angeles, 14, 24, 44, 55, 59, 64, 66,
    69, 76, 82, 102, 105, 106, 110, 112,
    129, 134, 136, 137, 147, 148, 151,
    156, 165
Los Angeles City College, 105
Los Angeles Theater Center, 106
Lou, Borromeo, 16
Lumbab, Ellery, 158
Lumbera, Bienvenido, 36
    Hibik at Himagsik nina Victoria
        Lactao [Victoria Lactao and the
        Women's Cry and Revolt], 36
Luna, Barbara, 38
Mabanglo, Ruth, 80
Mabesa, Antonio "Tony", 46, 53
    University of Delaware, 46
Macapugay, Jaygee, 55, 71
MacArthur Fellowship (Genius grant),
    107
Madama Butterfly, 102
Madjus, Jeigh, 162
Magic Theatre, 69
Magno-Hall, Deedee, 104
Magwili, Domingo "Dom" Albert, 48,
    63, 64, 81, 134
Magwili, Saachiko, 65
    Manila Murders, 63, 66
    Nobody On My Side of the Family
        Looks Like That!, 65
Majestic Theatre, 168
Malla, Carlos, 22
Manalo, Allan, 29, 74, 122, 134
Manhattan School of Music, 116
Manila, 5, 7, 10, 21, 22, 30, 31, 32, 35,
    36, 39, 45, 46, 47, 56, 57, 62, 63, 66,
    69, 84, 88, 93, 97, 102, 105, 106, 108,
    111, 115, 117, 118, 120, 122, 129,
    130, 132, 138, 145, 147, 153, 158,
    159, 163
Manila Serenaders, 22
Manila Swingsters, 22
Manila Symphony Society, 97
Manila Synchopators, 21
Manila Theatre Guild, 33, 118
Manila warriors, 6
Manilatown
    in San Diego, 68
    in San Francisco, 25
Manis, Potri Ranka, 118
Maog, Victor Malana, 136, 158
Mapa, Alec, 77
Marcos, Ferdinand, 54, 69, 71, 83

Marcos, Imelda, 55, 69, 71
    Cumpas, Estrella, 71
    Diaz, Ramona, 72
    Imelda (documentary film), 72
    Navarro-Pedrosa, Carmen, 72
    Untold Story of Imelda Marcos, The
        (book), 72
martial law, 54, 66, 69, 72, 83, 90, 93,
    105, 116, 121
Maryknoll Hall, 19
Mascarenas, Angela, 86, 99, 150, 165
Matilda, 168
Ma-Yi Theater Company, 24, 54, 76, 81,
    86, 93, 95, 96, 97, 107, 108, 115, 126,
    136, 137, 138, 139, 144, 149, 152,
    161, 163
    Abuan, Margot, 93
    Frilles, Anky, 93
    Garces, Chito Jao, 93
    Oca, Isolda, 93
    Ortoll, Jorge, 93
    Recto, Arianne, 93
    Savage Stage Plays By Ma-Yi
        Theater Company (book), 126
    Villanueva, Bernie, 93
Ma-Yi Writers Lab, 137, 164
    Rno, Sung, 137
McKinley, William, 7
McNally, Terrence, 98
    Love! Valour! Compassion!, 97
McTurk, David Harvey, 33
Mezclao Productions, 147
    Kalayaan, 147
    Kwentong Pinoy, 147
    Lazy Juan and the Bee Powder, 147
midget, 12
Midsummer Night's Dream, A, 163
Millado, Chris, 24, 85, 88, 90, 99, 111,
    126
    Buwan at Baril sa EB Major [Moon
        and Gun in EB Major], 96
    Nikimalika, 86
    Panata sa Kalayaan [Oath to
        Freedom], 85
    peregriNasyon [Wandering Nation],
        86, 92, 126, 151
    scenes from an unfinished country
        1905/1995, 86
Miller, Arthur, 45
    Death of a Salesman, 45
Milwaukee, 82, 104
Milwaukee Repertory Theater, 161
Minneapolis, 136, 159
Minnesota, 31
Minsa'y Isang Gamu gamo [Once a

Moth], 35
minstrel shows, 16
Mirza, Rehana Lew, 138
  Barriers, 138
  Mirza, Rohi, 138
  Soldier X, 138
Miss Saigon, 14, 77, 85, 102, 169
  Mackintosh, Cameron, 102
  Pryce, Jonathan, 102
  Schonberg, Claude-Michel, 102
Mission to (dit)Mars, 155
Modern Filipina, A, 12
  Araullo, Jesusa, 12
  Castillejo, Lino, 12
Monk, Meredith, 108
Monstress, 25
  Presenting … The Monstress!, 25
  Remember the I-Hotel, 25
Montalban, Paolo, 77
Montano, Severino, 32
  Arena Theater, 32
  Ladies and the Senator, The, 35
  Sabina, 35
Moon Crane Theatre Company, 132
Moonlight Serenaders, 22
Moore, Pony, 7
Moreno, Virginia, 35
  Bayaning Huwad [Straw Patriot], 35
moro-moro, 129
Mu Performing Arts, 136, 139, 159
Muriera, Ron, 91, 122
music
  hip hop, 92
  jazz, 16, 50, 92
  rhythm and blues, 50
music composition, 96
Music Man, The, 159
  76 Trombones (song), 159
musical, 8, 10, 14, 23, 37, 38, 39, 55, 68,
  70, 71, 77, 81, 84, 100, 102, 109, 117,
  121, 134, 147, 157, 162, 167, 168
  book musical, 37
  concept musical, 41
  jukebox musical, 126
  megamusical, 76
Muslim, 129, 138
Narciso, Filipina, 59
National Asian American Theater
  Company (NAATCO), 68, 87, 127,
  136, 148, 153, 164
  Eng, Richard, 87
National Asian American Theater
  conference, 136
National Endowment for the Arts, 42,
  54

National Federation of Filipino
  American Associations, 134
National New Play Network, 140
national tour, 39, 77, 103, 104, 117,
  145, 167, 168
Native American, 13, 43, 159
Nederlander Organization, 15
Negro Ensemble Company, 44
New Jersey, 30, 145, 149
New Playwright's Workshop, 132
New School, The, 153
New York City, 1, 10, 14, 15, 24, 38, 42,
  44, 46, 54, 56, 59, 63, 64, 72, 76, 93,
  95, 102, 107, 108, 110, 112, 127, 136,
  151, 158, 165
New York City Ballet, 168
New York International Fringe
  Festival, 113
New York Musical Theatre Festival,
  162
New York University, 77, 80, 86, 97,
  108, 112, 113, 138, 148, 152, 159,
  161, 170
Nibras Arab American Theater, 144
Nicholas Sengson
  Butil-Buhay [Grain-Life], 84
  *Ito Ang Pilipino [This is The
  Pilipino]*, 84
Night of the Iguana, The, 97
Noblezada, Eva, 104, 169
Noor Theatre, 145
Northwest Asian American Theatre
  (NWAAT), 24, 44, 62, 82
  Hongo, Garrett, 62
  Irigon, Yolly, 61
  Pacis, Gloria, 61
  Tokuda, Marilyn, 61
  Tonel, Henry, 61
  Wong, Larry, 61
Oberlin College, 108
Obispo, Fabian, 96, 157
Odets, Clifford, 127
  Awake and Sing!, 127
Off-Broadway
  industry, 42, 96, 97, 149
  production, 66, 69, 71, 165
  theater company, 95
Oh, Soon-Tek, 48
  Martyrs Can't Go Home, 48
  Tondemonai—Never Happen!, 48
Oklahoma!, 37
Old Globe Theatre, 99, 152
Old Vic, The, 152
Omaha, Nebraska, 6, 7
On The Town, 168

Once on This Island, 97, 168
One Flew Over the Cuckoo's Nest, 99
Ong, Han, 106, 126
   Airport Music, 107
   Bachelor Rat, 106
   Cornerstone Geography, 106
   In a Lonely Country, 106
   LA Plays, The, 106
   Middle Finger, 107, 122, 126
   Reason to Live. Half. No Reason, 106
   Savage Acts, 126
   Short List of Alternate Places, A, 107
   Swoony Planet, 107
   Symposium in Manila, 106
Onrubia, Cynthia, 68
opera, 9, 54, 76, 97, 99, 102
Oregon Shakespeare Festival, 99, 156
Orpheum circuit, 16
Ortega, Giovanni, 24, 71, 147
   Allos the story of Carlos Bulosan, 24, 148
   Criers for Hire, 148
Osias, Francisco "Frank", 22
Oxon Hill, Maryland, 168
Pabotoy, Orlando, 126, 151
Paglipas ng Dilim [After the Darkness Passes], 53
   Leon Ignacio, 53
   Palma, Precioso, 53
Pajama Game, The, 39
Palabas Essays on Philippine Theater (book), 3, 32
Palileo, Ruth Pe, 150
   High Stakes, 150
   Trinity College (Dublin), 150
Pamana [Heritage] (dance group), 110
Pamatmat, A. Rey, 139
   after all the terrible things I do, 140
   Deviant, 139
   Edith Can Shoot Things and Hit Them, 139
   House Rules, 140
   Thunder Above Deeps Below, 139
Pan Asian Repertory Theatre, 44, 67, 81, 87, 116, 136
Panganiban, Conrad, 24, 74, 141
   Esperanza Means Hope, 142
   Inay's Wedding Dress, 142
   Welga, 24
Panis, Alleluia, 91, 135
Paraiso, Nicky, 107
   Asian Boys, 107
   House/Boy, 107
   Houses and Jewels, 107
Parañaque City, 129

Pascasio, Louie, 100
Patrick, John, 39
   Teahouse of the August Moon, 39
Pazcoguin, Georgina, 168
PCN Salute, 74
Pearl of the Orient Dance Company, 21
Pearl Project, The, 146
Pecktal, Lynn, 97
   Costume Design Techniques of Modern Masters (book), 97
Peeling the Banana (Peeling), 112
   Kwong, Dan, 113
pejorative, 44, 94, 108
Peña, Ralph, 54, 62, 86, 93, 126, 161
   Project Balangiga, 126
Peñaranda, Oscar, 50, 63, 89, 122
   Followers of the Seasons, 63
   Truant, The, 63
Pensionado Act, 11, 12
People Of Interest, 152
   FAN stories from the brothels of Bangkok, 152
People Power Revolution, 71, 84, 85
Perez, Jason Magabo, 60
   Passion of El Hulk Hogancito, The, 60
   You Will Gonna Go Crazy, 60
Perez, Leonora, 59
Perseverance Theatre, 157
   Ellefson, Merry, 157
   Paparelli, Paul Joseph, 158
Phantom of the Opera, The, 76, 104, 168
Philadelphia, 136
Philippine Constabulary, 12
Philippine Daily Inquirer, 3, 55, 171
Philippine Dance Company of New York, 115
Philippine Educational Theater Association (PETA), 35, 45, 47, 55, 85, 86, 89, 91, 93, 99, 101, 116, 120, 122, 130
   Guidote, Bobby, 116
   Hermano, Rudy, 116
   Pacubas, Melvi, 116
   Pajaron, Ding, 116
Philippine Educational Theatre Arts League, 56, 81
   Kuwintas ni Lumnay [Lumnay's Necklace], 56
   Sundalo [Soldier], 56
Philippine Forum (activist group), 99
Philippine province
   Aklan, 22
   Antique, 150
   Bohol, 151

Cebu, 76, 97
Ilocos Norte, 52, 115
Ilocos Sur, 53
Iloilo, 19
Isabela, 52
Laguna, 40, 78
Leyte, 16, 48
Mountain Province, 111
Negros Occidental, 97
Quezon, 96
Philippine Theatre Davao, 31
Philippine Veterans' Band, 21
Philippine-American War, 7, 9, 10, 36,
    83, 121
Philippine insurrection, 7
Philippines
    commonwealth of USA, 26
    expatriates in, 33
    indigenous peoples, 8, 12
    nationalist wave, 34
Phillips, Lou Diamond, 116
Pilipino American Collegiate
    Endeavor, 43, 49, 122
Pilipino Artists Center, 63
Pilipino Cultural Night, 73, 88, 122, 141
Pimentel, Benjamin
    Mga Gerilya Sa Powell Street [The
        Guerillas of Powell Street]
        (book), 27
Ping Chong and Company, 112, 152
Pintig New Jersey [Pulse New Jersey],
    118
Pistahan, 92
Playwright Forum, 82
Playwrights' Arena, 55, 69, 105, 148,
    156, 164
Pohukaina School, 20
Poma, Edgar, 90, 158
    Little Train, 90, 158
Pomona College, 147
Porter, Cole, 30
Portland, 14
Portsmouth, Virginia, 104
Prelude to a Kiss, 97
priest, 19, 30
Prison Dancer, 162
Professional Performing Arts School
    (Florida), 167
Prospectus for the National Theater of
    the Philippines, A, 47
Prudencio, Jesca, 152
Public Theater, The (The Public), 69,
    71, 106, 108, 110, 152, 161
Puccini, Giacomo, 102
Puerto Rico, 7

Puro Arte Filipinos on the Stages of
    Empire (book), 3, 135
QBd Ink, 120
    Cabacungan, Remedios "Remy", 120
    Caparas, Bob, 120
    Garcia, Rod, 120
Quiniones, Marcus, 160
    Circle Around the Island, 160
Quintero, Wayland, 111
Quintos, Floy, 36
    and St. Louis loves dem Filipinos, 36
Quismorio, Alan, 133
Ramos, Clint, 169
Ramos, Teresita, 80
Randolph, Budd, 6
    Dewey in Manila, 6
Rebusit, Nancy, 24
regional theater, 42, 96, 159
Rent, 117
Repertory Philippines, 46, 93, 102, 103,
    132
Reuter, James Bertram, 30, 47, 56
revues, 16, 33
Reyes, Kristine, 147, 154
    Balikbayan Birthday, 155
    Lola Luning's First Steps, 155
    Quarter Century Baby, 147
    Queen for a Day, 154
    Something Blue, 147
Reyes, Randy, 136, 159
Reyes-Adan, Ricci, 56
Ricamora, Conrad, 71, 167
Rick Shiomi
    Yellow Fever, 68
Riggs, Arthur Stanley, 9
    Filipino Drama (book), 9
riots, 18
    Exeter, 18
    Los Angeles, 105
    Watsonville, 18
Rivera, Danny, 167
Rivera, Jon Lawrence, 54, 69, 105, 156,
    164
Rivera, Jose Lorenzo "Larry", 105
Rizal, Jose, 121
Rock of Ages, 167
Rodgers, Richard, 30, 37, 77
Rojo, Trinidad, 20
    Lights Off and a Double Surprise, 20
Roke, GD, 11
    Ang Sintang Dalisay ni Julieta at
        Romeo [Pure Love of Julieta and
        Romeo], 11
Rolling World Premiere, 140
Romance of Magno Rubio, The, 96, 126,

161
Romance of Magno Rubio, The (story),
23
Romasanta, Gayle, 133
Royal Hawaiian Band, 21
De los Santos, Francisco, 21
Inocencio, Geronimo, 21
Lebornio, Jose, 21
Salamanca, Lazaro, 21
Royal Serenaders, 21
Ruivivar, Francis, 104
Ryskamp, Kenneth, 98
Saint Paul College, 30, 31, 47, 120
Sakamoto, Edward, 49, 65
    That's the Way the Fortune Cookie
    Crumbles, 65
    Yellow is My Favorite Color, 49
Salonga, Lea, 47, 77, 102, 117, 168
Saludes, Pacita, 52
    Bullalayaw Ti Ayat [Love Is A
    Rainbow], 53
    Gapu Ta Patpatgenka [Because You
    Are Dear To Me], 52
    Uray Lakay No Landing [Even If
    He's Old When He Comes From
    Abroad], 53
San Angel, Gary, 112
San Diego, 51, 68, 69, 99, 109, 110, 134,
    142, 148, 149, 165
San Diego Asian American Repertory
    Theatre, 143
San Diego Playwrights, 142
San Dionisio sa America [San Dionisio
    in America], 129
    Ang Kambal ng Valencia [The Twins
    of Valencia], 131
    Esperanza at Caridad [Esperanza
    and Caridad], 131
    Hermano de la Paz, 131
    Herpacio, Joseph, 130
    Mga Prinsesa ng Cordova [The
    Princesses of Cordova], 131
    Nerissa at Bolivar [Nerissa and
    Bolivar], 131
    San Agustin, Rick, 130
San Francisco, 14, 16, 22, 23, 24, 25, 28,
    43, 44, 49, 59, 60, 62, 64, 68, 69, 76,
    79, 82, 86, 89, 90, 91, 106, 108, 114,
    122, 123, 134, 139, 145, 148, 153,
    165
San Francisco Ethnic Dance Festival,
    63
San Francisco Mime Troupe, 91
San Francisco State (school), 43, 49,
    122

San Jose State University, 78
San Jose, Sean, 25, 114
    Pieces of the Quilt, 114
Sarah Lawrence College, 68, 155
sarsuwela, 8, 21, 22, 36, 37, 52, 53, 119
scholarship, 40, 47, 85, 119, 159, 170
    Fulbright Program, 32
    Rockefeller Foundation, 32
Search to Involve Pilipino Americans,
    147
Seattle, 14, 19, 20, 22, 24, 31, 44, 51, 59,
    60, 82, 86, 109, 167
Seattle College, 19
Seattle Repertory Theater, 20
Second Generation, 136, 139, 158
Sedition Act, 8
seditious plays, 9, 37, 86
    Abad, Juan, 9
    Kahapon, Ngayon at Bukas
    [Yesterday, Today and
    Tomorrow], 9
    Tanikalang Guinto [Golden Chain], 9
    Tolentino, Aurelio, 9
See, Chester, 167
Sengson, Nicholas, 84, 120
    Hanap Mula [Always Searching],
    120
    Yambao, Jaime, 120
Serban, Andrei, 115
    Greek Trilogy, 115
Seril, Bruna, 115
set design, 97
    plagiarism case, 97
Shakespeare, William, 11, 30, 36, 163
    Julius Caesar, 11, 30
    Merchant of Venice, The, 11
    Romeo and Juliet, 11
    Taming of the Shrew, The, 36
Shiomi, Rick, 68, 160
Shoo Fly Regiment, 10
    Cole, Bob, 10
    Down in the Philippines (song), 10
    Johnson, John Rosamond, 10
    On the Gay Luneta (song), 10
Shubert Organization, 15
Sicangco, Eduarto "Toto", 97
Sinag-tala Filipino Theater and
    Performing Arts Association, 141
Sining Bayan [People's Art], 57, 85
    Frame-up of Narciso and Perez, The,
    59
    Isuda ti Immuna [Those Who Were
    First], 58
    Maguindanao, 58
    Mindanao, 58

Occena, Bruce, 57
Silva, John, 57
Tagatupad [Those Who Must Carry
    On], 58
Ti Mangyuna [Those Who Led the
    Way], 59
War Brides, 59
Sining KilUSAn [Art Movement], 109
Carrillo, Manuel, 109
Cordova, Damian, 110
Pizarro, Angelo, 110
Salvador, Ramon, 109, 110
Sison, Joel, 110
Sison, Cristina, 93, 95
Slant, 112
Big Dicks, Asian Men, 112
Ebihara, Richard, 112
Yung, Perry, 112
Sledgehammer Theatre, 99
Smith, Jacob, 100
Sondheim, Stephen, 67
Pacific Overtures, 67
sound design, 96
Sound of Music, 117
South Pacific, 38
Spanish-American War, 5, 6
St. John, Betta, 38
St. Louis, Missouri, 12
Sta. Ana, Lianah, 169
stage management, 95, 97
Stanislavski, Konstantin, 15
stereotype, 14, 44, 87, 112
Stevens, Thomas Woods, 78
Stewart, Ellen, 55
stock theater company, 15, 30
Streetcar Named Desire, A, 99
Streets of All Nations, 6
Strindberg, August, 46
Miss Julie, 46
Sullivan, Arthur, 30, 75
Summer Theatre Arts Repertory (STAR
    Arts Education), 78
Sundance Theater Laboratory, 109
Swados, Elizabeth, 115
Swanbeck, Alex, 56
Pet for Company, 56
Syquia, Luis "Lou", 50, 89
Taft, William Howard, 7
Taleon-Sonza, Jorshinelle, 146, 153
Cold Flesh, 154
Dog Days in America and Other
    Plays (book), 154
Drew University, 153
Encounter, The, 146
Haiyan and Other Plays about the

Homeland (book), 154
How to Cook Adobo, 153
Lena's Way, 154
Migration Blues, 153
Sandman, 153
Tandy Beal and Company, 112
Tanghalan Repertory Theatre
    [Performance Repertory Theatre],
    53
Tanghalang Pilipino ng DC [Pilipino
    Theater of DC], 84, 119, 120
Bangit, Elvi, 84
Bangit, Rey, 84
Bayan Ko Bumangon Ka [My
    Country Rise], 84
Brooks, George, 84
EDSA!, 84
Jumat, Boots, 84
Jumat, Gerry, 84
Lopez, Gabby, 84
Melegrito, Elvie, 84
Melegrito, Jonathan "Jon", 84
Tagle, Luis Antonio "Chito", 84
Tanglao-Aguas, Francis, 131
Abuja Woman, 131
Ramayana La'ar, 131
Sarimanok Travels, The, 131
When the Purple Settles, 131
Where the Carabao Sleeps, 131
Teatro Campesino, El, 44, 58, 78, 92
Teatro ng Tanan (TnT) [Theater for
    Everyone], 89, 93, 122, 123, 133,
    134, 140, 158
Aguinaldo, Edgar, 89
Camagong, Julia, 89
Consul, Wilma, 134
Estrada, Mars, 89
Kin Kamag-Anak, 89
Marasigan, Marlette, 89
Marasigan, Marnelle "Bingo", 89
Marasigan, Violeta "Bullet", 90
Panunuluyan [Seeking Shelter], 91
Tabios, Presco, 89
Torres, Alex, 89
Torres, Mara, 89
Teatro Pilipino. See Tanghalang
    Pilipino ng DC [Pilipino Theater of
    DC]
television
    adapted for, 77
    working in, 40, 77, 78, 103, 104
Tenorio, Lysley, 25
Theater Underground (University of
    California Los Angeles), 131
TheaterMania.com, 113

TheaterWorks, 83, 92
Theatre Arts Project (San Joaquin
    County), 159
Theatre Communications Group (TCG),
    42, 64, 136, 160
    New Generations Future Leaders
    Mentorship grant, 160
Theatre Unlimited, 67
Theatrical Ensemble of Asians. *See*
    Northwest Asian American Theatre
    (NWAAT)
Theatrical Syndicate, 15
Third World Institute of Theatre Arts
    Studies, 57, 68, 97
Third World Liberation Front, 43
Thunder Mountain Theatre Project.
    See Generator Theater Company
tinikling, 92
Tinio, Rolando, 45
    State University of Iowa, 45
    Teatro Pilipino (Manila), 45
Tiongco, Maureen, 40
Tiongson, Nicanor, 36
    Pilipinas Circa 1907, 36
Tolentino, Jhett, 166
    *Gentleman's Guide to Love and
        Murder, A*, 166
    Raffe, Joan, 166
    Raisin in the Sun, A, 166
    *Vanya and Sonia and Masha and
        Spike*, 166
tongue in A mood, 74, 122, 134
    Cachapero, Patty, 123
    Camia, Kevin, 123
    Gonzales, Ogie, 123
    Kabasares, Kennedy, 122
    Navarette, Rex, 122
touring theater company, 15
Towards A Cultural Community
    Identity, Education and
    Stewardship in Filipino American
    Performing Arts (publication), 135
Treaty of Manila (1946), 26
Treaty of Paris (1898), 6
Trimillos, Ricardo "Ric", 53
Trinidad, Hana, 110
Tropang Bodabil [Bodabil Troupe]
    (Peryante), 85, 86, 89, 93
Tsunami Theatre, 157
    Taylor, Joan Rebecca, 157
Tydings-McDuffie Act (1934), 18, 26
    Filipino Exclusion Act, 18
    Philippine Independence Act, 26
United Nations, 56, 57
    UNESCO, 56

United Scenic Artists, 98
University of California
    Berkeley, 14, 27, 43, 44, 57, 88
    Davis, 79
    Irvine, 149
    Los Angeles, 46, 131, 143, 147, 153
    San Diego, 99, 148, 152
    Santa Barbara, 53
University of Chicago, 31
    Godwin Theatre School, 31
University of Hawaii, 20, 45, 46, 52, 78,
    80, 110, 132
    Filipino and Philippine Literature
        program, 80
    Ilocano Language Program, 52
University of Kansas, 66, 80, 128
University of Notre Dame du Lac, 131
University of San Francisco, 64
University of Southern California, 156
University of the Arts (Philadelphia),
    137, 148
University of the Philippines, 31, 36,
    46, 93, 132
    Dulaang Unibersidad ng Pilipinas
        (DUP), 36, 46, 132
    UP Dramatic Club, 31, 40
    UP Madrigal Singers, 96, 118
    UP Repertory Company, 46
University of Utah, 159
University of Virginia, 160
University of Washington, 20, 31, 51,
    61
US Bureau of Educational and Cultural
    Affairs, 32
US Coast and Geodetic Survey, 19
US Naval Auxiliary Force, 9
US Navy, 26, 53
Valdes-Aran, Ching, 95, 115
    Ilocana, 115
Valdes-Lim, Ana, 110
    Assumption College, 111
    Marie Eugenie Theater of the
        Assumption, 111
    Philippine Playhouse, 111
Valdez, Luis, 51
    Los Vendidos [*The Sold Ones*], 51
Valentin, Orlando, 21
Valentin, Priscilla "Pat", 21
Valentin, Rafaela Pandaraoan, 20
    Pantomima de Amor [*Love
        Pantomime*], 21
Vance, Charles, 118
vaudeville, 16, 33
    political vaudeville, 85
Velasco, Lorna Aquino Chui, 28, 123,

163
Vera, Rodolfo "Rody", 27, 100
    Alamat [Legends], 100
    Bells of Balangiga, 100
    Guerrillas of Powell Street, The, 27
Versace, Gianni, 109
veterans (war)
    Equity Bill, 28
    Rescission Act (1946), 27
    Veterans Administration hospital,
        59
    Vietnam War, 58, 62
    Viray, Francisco, 28
    World War II, 27
Vietnam War, 43, 62, 102
    Vietnam Memorial, 83
Villa, Jose Garcia, 53, 81
    Mir I Nisa, 53
Village Voice, The, 42, 128
Vinluan, Ermena Marlene, 57
Virgin Labfest, 163
vod-a-vil. See bodabil
Vortex Theatre Company, 139
Voyage, 158
Waltham, Massachusetts, 157
Washington Shakespeare Company,
    121
Washington, DC, 35, 46, 59, 66, 67, 83,
    84, 86, 96, 110, 116, 118, 119, 121,
    131, 134, 137, 157
Wedekind, Frank, 107

Spring Awakening, 107
West End, 102
West Side Story, 39, 117
Wicked, 104, 167
William Morris Agency, 66
Williams, Tennessee, 45
    Glass Menagerie, The, 45
Wing, Arlene, 22
Wing, Tony, 22
Women of Color Productions, 155
Wonderland Alice's New Musical
    Adventure, 117
Wong, Bradley Darryl "BD", 76
World Trade Center, 125, 138
World War I, 16
World War II, 26, 30, 33, 34, 38, 39, 56,
    58, 92, 118, 168
    Filipino Infantry Regiments, 26
    US Armed Forces in the Far East
        (USAFFE), 26, 27
Yale Repertory Theater, 152
Yale University, 32, 78, 139, 149, 160,
    161
Yerba Buena Center for the Arts, 92
Yew, Chay, 157
    Long Season, The, 157
Young Playwrights Festival, 138
zarzuela, 8, See also sarsuwela
Ziegfeld Follies, 16
Zulueta, Ogie, 69

About the author

Walter Ang writes about Filipino American theater for Inquirer.net and Philippine Daily Inquirer.

Feedback for *Barangay to Broadway: Filipino American Theater History* can be sent to filipinoamericantheater@gmail.com.

Made in the USA
Las Vegas, NV
12 December 2023